THE REAL BOOK ABOUT

DANIEL BOONE

This book belongs too Roger Hesseltine, given to him by his mother on his eleventh Birthday.

THE REAL BOOK ABOUT

DANIEL BOONE

By

William Cunningham

Illustrated by

DEANE CATE

EDITED BY HELEN HOKE

Garden City Books

GARDEN CITY, NEW YORK

BY ARRANGEMENT WITH FRANKLIN WATTS, INC.

1952
GARDEN CITY BOOKS

PRINTED IN THE UNITED STATES
AT THE COUNTRY LIFE PRESS, GARDEN CITY, N.Y.
FIRST EDITION

CONTENTS

ACKNOWLEDGMENT

I wish to thank John Bakeless for reading this manuscript and making many helpful suggestions. Mr. Bakeless is author of the authoritative work, DANIEL BOONE, MASTER OF THE WILDERNESS.

THE AUTHOR

THE *REAL BOOK* ABOUT

DANIEL BOONE

1

WARRIORS IN THE PASTURE

When Daniel Boone was a boy he played Indian with real Indians who carried tomahawks and long rifles.

In the spring of 1744, when he was nine and a half years old, his father bought a piece of pasture land several miles from the Boone farm in Pennsylvania. The cows could not be driven from the farm to the new land and back again every day, so Daniel's father built a log cabin beside a spring in the pasture and Daniel and his mother moved out there to live during the summer months.

Daniel's job was to watch the cows and drive them to the cabin each day at sunset for milking. But cows do not need close watching, so he was free to wander and explore in the deep woods. This arrangement suited him just fine. He felt it was much better to explore than to work in the corn patch back at the farm.

He was still too young to carry a gun, but he made himself a throwing spear from a hickory stick. After long practice, he became such a good spear thrower that he could sometimes kill small game. Often to test his skill he stalked a bear or a deer, although of course he could not kill big game with a spear made from a hickory stick.

One morning at sunrise he left the cows in a glade where the grass was good and noted carefully how the wind was blowing, so he could easily find them again. Cows and other animals wandering in the woods keep their faces to the wind so they can catch the scent of things ahead of them. He judged the herd would graze down toward Flying Hill.

Flying Hill did not really fly. But when anyone went there, so many wild turkeys took to the air that it seemed the whole top of the hill was flying away.

Off in another direction a crow called. Daniel could not see the crow, but he knew it was sitting at the top of a tree as a sentry for other crows far or near.

He decided to play that he was an Indian scout in dangerous territory and this crow was the lookout for a band of enemy warriors. If he could creep to within shooting range of the crow without letting the crow see him, it would prove that he was a good scout. He started toward the crow.

He did not go swinging along the easiest path, crashing through dry leaves, stepping on sticks, and otherwise making a commotion. Instead, he kept close to the bushes, crouching low, watching where he put his feet, stopping to listen every few steps.

He was dressed in homespun trousers and deerskin jacket and moccasins so that he was the color of the brown earth and the dead leaves. When he faded into a thicket and lay motionless, he was invisible. When he had to cross an open space, he crawled or made a swift run, crouching low.

He kept his eyes constantly on the ground in front of him, looking not only for tracks but also for sluggish, fat snakes. Swift-running snakes were harmless and kept out of the way, but fat, slow ones were usually dangerous and the penalty for stepping on one might be death. He also watched overhead for birds and noted what the squirrels were doing on high branches.

Meanwhile, Daniel's ears were as busy as his eyes. They told him what was going on a hundred yards or a quarter of a mile ahead. In the deep forest, birds and small animals keep each other informed of what they see. Although they have no words, they can make themselves understood by their tone of voice. Calm chatter and chirps and croaks mean all is well. Angry scolding means they have found a snake or owl or some other despised thing which steals eggs and eats nestlings. Shrill cries of fright or sometimes dead silence means the animals or birds see something big and dangerous, such as a man or a lynx.

Crows are the best informers, because they are not only the wisest of birds but also the noisiest—unless of course they are engaged in a little thievery of their own in the corn patch.

On this day, as Daniel crept along, the crow ahead of him talked calmly.

To the woodsman, a patch of soft ground beside a pool or stream is like a newspaper telling what has happened recently hereabouts. Now Daniel came to soft ground and read some news which interested him. Big bear tracks and little bear tracks told him that a mother bear and her cubs had been here.

Unless you have a gun and want bear steak, there is no point in trailing a lone papa bear. When you find him he just stands up and stares at you and then lumbers off.

He does not want trouble or any truck with the likes of you.

But a mama bear with cubs is different. She will stand her ground or even charge if you get too close. Then you have to climb a small tree. A bear must hug a tree to climb and therefore cannot follow you up the tree if the trunk is too small to hug.

Daniel knew all this and it gave him an idea. Perhaps he could climb a big tree and encourage the bear to follow. Then he could go out on a high limb and jump into the top of a small tree and scramble down and run. It would be a new way to get away from a bear. He had never been treed by a bear, but a few days before he had tried jumping from a big tree into the top of a smaller one. The limbs of the small tree bent and let him down to the ground without a scratch.

For a moment Daniel considered taking up this trail and trying to find the bear family, just to see what would happen. Then he saw a deer track on top of a cub track. This meant the tracks were not fresh, maybe days old. Disappointed, he resumed his game with the sentry crow.

He could not see the crow, for he must always keep bushes and tree trunks between him and it, but his ears told him that it was not far away, in a treetop on top of a hill.

Suddenly the crow squawked and flapped into the air. Daniel froze in his tracks, thinking the crow had caught a glimpse of him. But it did not circle over him as it would have done if it had seen him. Instead it sailed about a hundred yards and settled again out of his sight. This meant it had seen something else, on the other side of the hill.

Squirrels on top of the hill had been chattering and rustling among the leaves on the ground. Now they raced to their trees, climbed high, and flattened themselves on branches, keeping very still. They too had seen something.

Squirrels and crows are not afraid of bears or deers. There must be a man, or men, on the other side. At this season white men would be busy with their crops. Suddenly Daniel's game became deadly serious.

Not far north, beyond a range of low mountains, were several wigwam villages of the Delaware Indians. White people of this region had always treated the Indians fairly, and the Delawares were friendly. But far to the west lived other, unknown tribes.

Sometimes white desperadoes crossed the mountains into this western land and raided Indian villages, killing men, women and children, and taking valuable furs, horses and other property. Then warriors from these wild tribes came east to get revenge and fell upon white settlements without warning. There had been no Indian trouble in this part of Pennsylvania for a long time, but Daniel knew that such a raid was possible.

He had to get to the top of the hill and see what he could see. If he spied strange Indians, painted for war, he must race back to the cabin to warn his mother—or die in the attempt. Daniel knew that when Indians went on the warpath, they decorated their faces and bodies with red and black paint.

The best route to the top of the hill led past where the crow was calling. If Daniel went that way, the crow would see him and circle over him, cawing with new alarm, and the Indians would spot him.

There was no time to lose. Daniel crouched low and ran to the top of the hill by a longer route. Only the squirrels saw him and they kept still, as he knew they would.

He crawled into a thicket and watched. In a little while his eyes caught a movement of the bushes beside a creek. A tall Indian, carrying a long rifle, appeared. His scalp lock stood up stiffly from his brown head. Other warriors followed, walking in single file along a deer path. They were Delawares and wore white paint, which meant they were at peace. There was no cause for alarm.

Probably they were on their way to his father's blacksmith shop to have a gun repaired and hold a friendly powwow.

Daniel was greatly relieved. He was also rather pleased with himself, to think that he could scout well enough to spy on Indians, even the friendly Delawares, without being seen. They had keen eyes and ears. If he had made a small mistake, they would have seen him.

There was good cover along the top of the hill, and Daniel decided to keep the Indians in sight for a while. That would be good practice. When the last warrior had passed, he stood up and slipped through the bushes, ready to freeze if one of them looked back. He did not make a sound. Trailing Indians, he found, was not as hard as he thought it would be.

Suddenly right in front of him he saw a patch of tan hide, then the large, beautiful eyes of a deer. Evidently the deer had been watching the Indians and now was startled to discover a man, or almost a man, right beside it. The deer crashed through the bushes and raced away as Daniel fell on his face.

One of the warriors grunted sharply and raised his

Daniel saw warriors walking single file along a deer path

rifle. The others stopped. But when they saw the deer, they decided that it alone was responsible for the commotion. They were not hunting deer, so they walked on.

For a long time, Daniel lay in the bushes thinking. He had made a bad mistake. Looking so hard at the Indians, he had forgotten to watch the bushes right in front of him. A good scout watches everything. Suppose, instead of the deer, he had blundered into the mother bear with cubs, and no tree within reach. He decided he still had much to learn.

2

DANIEL'S EDUCATION

Daniel Boone was born November 2, 1734, in Oley Township, now Berks County, Pennsylvania. His father, Squire Boone, a fiery little man, was a farmer, weaver, blacksmith, and hunter. His mother was a gentle, quiet woman, tall with dark hair, who seldom scolded her many children and never complained of the hardships of pioneer life. Daniel was their sixth child.

The Boone cabin stood in a clearing in the tall woods. Nearby were cabins of other pioneer families. Daniel made his first explorations in his father's blacksmith shop, in the cornfield, and in the cabins and barns of the neighbors.

He and his sister Elizabeth, two years older, watched the sparks fly when their father pounded a piece of red-hot iron. They went to the edge of the woods and played they were hunters, or they raced down the road to a cabin where other children lived and pretended they were wild Indians from across the mountains attacking a white settlement.

One summer when Daniel was about four, the children in a nearby cabin came down with smallpox. Daniel's mother told him and Elizabeth that they must stay at home until the epidemic was over. They could not even go to the blacksmith shop, for fear they would meet someone who carried the pox on his clothes.

Daniel was very unhappy. He loved freedom. There was nothing to do in the Boone cabin except watch his mother run a spinning wheel or his older brother operate a big clanking loom which made cloth. He talked it over with Elizabeth.

"If we could get the pox," he said, "we would be sick for a little while. But after that we would never catch it again, and mother would let us go where we pleased."

Elizabeth agreed that it would be nice to have smallpox. They made plans.

That night they crept out of the Boone cabin without a sound, ran to the neighbor's cabin, and got in bed with one of their friends who was sick. Then they ran back home. Nobody saw them.

A few days later they took sick and were very pleased about it. However, their mother guessed that they were expecting this sickness.

"Daniel," she said, "I want thee to tell thy mother the truth."

The Boones were Quakers and used the old words "thee" and "thy" instead of "you" and "your."

Daniel told the truth.

His mother was distressed, but she did not become angry. She explained to him that he had done a foolish thing. Then she added, "Thee should have told me sooner, so that I could be prepared."

All seven Boone children, from Sara, aged fourteen, to Mary, aged two, had the smallpox, but fortunately none of them got very sick. Soon Daniel and Elizabeth were again able to explore.

Probably about this time Daniel made up his mind to be a hunter, rather than a farmer, weaver, or blacksmith, because a hunter does not have to stay at home.

On the frontier, hunting was a most important job. A family needed little corn if it had plenty of fresh meat. Bearhides and deerskins could be traded for "store-bought" goods. The skin of a buck deer was worth a dollar, and pioneers often used buckskins instead of coins. To this day people sometimes call a dollar a "buck," not knowing they are using the language of Daniel's time. Doe skins were also used in exchange and this is probably the origin of the slang word "dough" meaning money.

As soon as his legs were long enough, Daniel trotted after his father and older brothers when they went deer hunting. On a day when a hunt was planned, Daniel was the first one up. Leaping from his warm bearskin bed, he shivered into buckskin trousers and rawhide boots which were as stiff as boards from their wetting of the day before. Breaking a layer of ice on the bucket, he splashed water into a wooden basin and washed his face. Then he bundled himself in a bearskin coat and was ready to go, forgetting that he had not had breakfast.

On the other hand, he could hardly drag himself out of bed on a warm summer morning if he faced a day of hoeing corn in the clearing.

Daniel's father realized that the boy was not cut out to be a farmer or weaver, so he set about making a hunter out of him. As soon as Daniel was big enough to aim a long rifle by resting the barrel on a stump or fallen tree trunk, his father taught him to shoot. On long hunting trips, his father explained to him the ways of deer, bear, squirrels, and wild turkey and told him how to load the gun for each of them. Daniel learned how to tell directions in a pathless forest, how to make a comfortable camp and kindle a fire while a freezing rain was falling.

When, at the age of nine and a half, he was given the wonderful job of herding cows in the far pasture, he was already an accomplished woodsman.

Anything that had to do with hunting or roaming the woods, Daniel learned very quickly. Other things he learned slowly or not at all.

He was good at making deerskin hunting shirts and moccasins but awkward at operating a loom which made cloth for Sunday-go-to-meeting clothes. He liked to repair guns in the blacksmith shop but not to sharpen plowshares. It is known that in later years he made beautiful powder horns, from cow horns, polishing and scraping them so thin that the separate grains of powder could be seen through the horn. He probably learned this art as a boy.

When he was twelve years old, his father gave him a rifle, and he was the happiest boy on the frontier.

The rifle was longer than he was, but by straining every muscle he could aim it without a rest. When it went off, he sometimes had to take a few steps backward to regain his balance, because it had a powerful kick. But after a few weeks of practice, he could shoot as well as his older brothers. At stalking game he was even better than they because he was more patient and careful.

The frontier rifle of those days was over five feet long and weighed around eleven pounds. A little piece of flint rock was attached to the hammer and held in place by setscrews.

To load such a rifle you carefully measured the right amount of powder and poured it into the muzzle—the front end—of the gun. Then you placed a little patch of home-made linen, with grease on it, in the muzzle. On the patch you put a round lead bullet the size of a small marble. Then you pushed the bullet and the patch down the barrel with a ramrod until the linen rested lightly on the powder. Next you put a pinch of powder in a tiny pan beneath the hammer, and you were ready to shoot.

When you pulled the trigger, the hammer came down and the flint scraped against a steel plate. Sparks flew and lighted the powder in the pan. Fire went through a tiny hole in the barrel to the powder charge. There was a bang, and a cloud of white smoke hid your target from view.

Compared with modern rifles, these guns were large and clumsy. Long practice was required to load them properly. But they were the best guns in the world at that time—far better, for instance, than the smooth-bore muskets used by the redcoats later during the Revolution. They were as accurate as are modern rifles.

Daniel named his new rifle "Tick-Licker," probably because the hammer said "tick-lick" when it was pulled back.

From dawn until dusk Daniel was in the woods. After supper, by the light of a tallow dip, he cleaned Tick-Licker and hung it on the wall. Then he molded some bullets, refilled his powder horn, and crawled into bed, to dream of hunting and exploring.

If Daniel ever went to school, it was only for a few

weeks or months. Pioneer settlements in those times seldom had schools. When he was fourteen or fifteen, the wife of his older brother taught him to read and write, add and divide. Arithmetic was easy because surveyors used arithmetic and Daniel thought of becoming a surveyor in the west. Spelling, however, was difficult. He could not see any reason why a hunter and explorer should bother his head with spelling. Throughout his life he spelled by ear. A bear was always a "bar" to him, and sometimes he even spelled his name "Boon."

Daniel's father was not disturbed by Daniel's inability to spell. "Let the gals do the spelling and Dan will do the shooting," he said.

Spelling was not as important in those days as it is now. George Washington, who lived at the same time, sometimes had difficulty with spelling although he was well educated in other ways.

3

TALK OF "BLOODY GROUND"

By the time Daniel was fifteen years old, it was hard to find a deer in the woods of Oley Township. Flying Hill no longer seemed to fly away when a hunter approached. Daniel's father felt that there were too many people and not enough game.

In the spring of 1750 he sold his farm and blacksmith shop, bought covered wagons, horses, and cattle, and started southwest. His whole family went along, except the two oldest boys who had already married and settled down.

The Boones were in no hurry and did not know exactly where they were going. When they found good pasture they camped for weeks to let the livestock graze. Daniel hunted to keep the family supplied with fresh meat. This was just the sort of life he liked. He could explore every day.

For nearly two years they wandered along the eastern edge of the mountains, through western Virginia and down into North Carolina. Here in the Yadkin Valley they found what they wanted—plenty of game and few hunters, so Daniel's father bought a farm on the Yadkin River. Daniel took to the woods with his Tick-Licker.

At first the hunting was too good to be any fun. He could kill twenty or thirty deer in one day. Then he had to spend several days "jerking" the meat—cutting it into thin slices to dry in the sun. He also had to salt down the skins and take them to market in the nearby town of Salisbury.

But such hunting could not last long. Soon he had to wander up into the Blue Ridge Mountains to find game. He knew the time would come even in this great country when a man could not hunt for a living but would have to farm. He wondered where he could go when that time came.

The friendly Catawba Indians who lived in the valley said that far to the northwest, beyond three ranges of mountains, there was a rich country called "Ken-ta-ke," which meant "the old fields." It was a "dark and bloody ground," they said. The powerful Cherokee tribe lived south of it, and the fierce Shawnees to the north.

Both tribes claimed Ken-ta-ke, but neither dared to settle there for fear of the other. It was a hunting ground and a battlefield. Each summer the ground was stained with the blood of Cherokee and Shawnee warriors.

Game was so abundant there, they said, that a man could sit beside a salt lick and kill deer, bear, and buffalo as fast as he could reload. Great herds of buffalo grazed on the plains, and their hoofs made a rumble like distant thunder. The woods were full of wild turkey. Along the river banks, cane grew twenty or thirty feet high.

White settlers in the Yadkin Valley also talked about "Caintuck," as they called it. But none of them had been there or planned to go. It was said that a white man would get an arrow through him before he ever set foot on the "dark and bloody ground."

Some of the old hunters had heard that the snakes in Caintuck had stingers on the ends of their tails. They rolled themselves up into hoops and chased deer. When they got up enough speed, they bounced into the air and straightened out and sailed like arrows, tail first. If they stuck their tails into anything, even a tree, it would swell up and burst.

Daniel did not believe everything he heard.

But he wanted to see Caintuck with his own eyes. Everything else seemed tame by comparison. Someday he would go there. But for a trip like that he needed packhorses, several rifles, lots of ammunition. He would have to be away from home for months, maybe years. If he had a farm of his own and sons to take care of it while he was gone, he could do some real exploring.

At the age of twenty-one, Daniel was five feet eight inches tall, with broad shoulders, thick chest, and narrow hips. His hair was moderately black, and his eyes were blue beneath yellowish eyebrows. He had a Roman nose, thin lips, a wide mouth and ruddy skin.

He spent most of his time alone, going on long hunts in the mountains, but he liked to be with people and he attended all neighborhood gatherings. He gained a local reputation as a wrestler, runner, and jumper.

Among the Indians was a young Catawba warrior, named Saucy Jack, who did not relish being beaten at shooting matches. He let it be known that he intended to kill Daniel. While Daniel was away on a hunting trip, the Boone family learned of this threat. When Daniel's father heard of it, he became so angry that he picked up a

An old hunter told tall tales about the snakes in "Caintuck"

hatchet and started looking for Saucy Jack. Saucy Jack, however, must have been warned, for he left the valley in a hurry, and nothing more was heard of his threat to Daniel.

Daniel's first big adventure occurred in 1755, shortly before his twenty-first birthday.

The French had built a fort, called Duquesne, in western Pennsylvania, where Pittsburgh now stands, and were encouraging the Indians to attack frontier settlements. General Braddock of the British Army came to America and with a force of British regulars and American militia marched into the wilderness toward the French fort to put a stop to these frontier assaults. With Braddock was young George Washington commanding the Virginia militia.

Daniel Boone, who was about two years younger than Washington, got a job driving a supply wagon for a detachment of North Carolina militia, who were also in the Braddock expedition. There is no evidence, though, that Boone and Washington got acquainted on this trip, although they probably met in later years.

But Daniel did meet a most interesting man—young John Finley, who had actually been to Kentucky. Finley had gone into Cherokee territory to trade, and a party of Cherokees took him into the "dark and bloody ground." Finley told Boone that Caintuck was a wonderful place. He had seen great herds of buffalo, and the woods were full of game.

"I want to go there myself some day," Daniel said. "I'm a hunter."

"The Indians won't let you hunt there," Finley explained. "They did not mind if I went along as a trader, but they wouldn't let me kill game for myself."

"Now that you've been there and know the way, you could go without the Indians, and keep out of their sight," Daniel suggested.

"I'm no woodsman," Finley confessed. "I get lost in the woods. The Indians would soon catch me."

"I don't get lost," Daniel said, "and I think I could hide from the Indians. Let's go together when this job is over."

"I'd like to do that," Finley agreed.

The job ended sooner than they expected. One day, as Braddock's forces approached Fort Duquesne, Daniel heard shots far ahead. Fighting had started. The wagon train halted. Then the roar of battle grew louder. Evidently there was plenty of trouble up ahead. The French and Indians were making a real fight.

Suddenly a party of warriors attacked the wagons just ahead of Daniel. He had no gun. No British soldiers or militia appeared to protect the wagons. Daniel jumped on one of the horses, slashed the tugs and rode for his life, as did the other wagoners.

A few months later he was back in the Yadkin Valley. He did not know what had become of his friend John Finley, and the trip to Caintuck seemed an impossible dream. Even the Yadkin Valley was no longer safe from Indian raids.

Daniel might have been very unhappy at this time, except that he fell in love. She was Rebecca Bryan, daughter of a farmer who lived near the Boones. Rebecca was rather tall, with dark hair and eyes. She was only sixteen, but people married young in those days.

Daniel wanted to be sure that she had a sweet temper. One day when he went to see her, she wore a white cambric apron of which any frontier girl would have been proud. She sat down on the grass and Daniel lounged beside her. He took out his hunting knife and began absent-mindedly slashing at blades of grass. Suddenly the knife slipped, accidentally—on purpose—and cut a hole in the apron. Rebecca did not lose her temper.

They were married in August, 1756, and settled down in a cabin on Daniel's father's farm. Less than three years later they had to flee to Culpeper County, Virginia, because of Indian raids. Here Daniel may have met George Washington. However, in October, 1759, they came back to the Yadkin Valley.

For ten years Daniel lived quietly, farming in summer and hunting in fall, spring, and winter. Sometimes he ranged far. In the mountains of eastern Tennessee he cut in the bark of a tree the words, "D. Boon cilled a Bar on Tree in the year 1760."

Probably when he carved the letters he was lonely and hoped that sometime, by accident, some other lonely hunter would see the words, possibly someone from the Yadkin Valley who knew him. He did not guess that this tree would stand for a hundred years and his inscription would be printed in millions of books.

His oldest son, James, was born in 1757. Eight years later, Daniel started taking James with him on long hunts and teaching him the ways of animals who live in the woods. When they were caught in a storm, Daniel would tuck the boy inside his hunting shirt to keep him from freezing. The hunting shirt of those days was a big, loose garment of deerskin, more like a modern overcoat than a shirt.

Daniel had not forgotten his desire to explore Kentucky. In fact he was saving money and making plans for such an adventure. Often he thought of the young trader John Finley and the plans they had made when they were driving wagons behind Braddock's army. He wondered what had become of John.

Daniel talked it over with his neighbors and relatives. They urged him to go because they wanted to leave North Carolina and find a better place to settle down. Game was scarce and crops were poor, and in addition, the governor of North Carolina, appointed by the King of England, forced them to pay high taxes. They wanted to find a new frontier, where they would be prosperous and free.

Daniel's younger brother, Squire Boone, jr., wanted to go with Daniel. Squire was a daring man, a good hunter and almost as good a woodsman as Daniel himself. John Stuart, Daniel's brother-in-law, also wanted to go. Stuart was Boone's close friend and they often went on hunts together.

One day in the early spring of 1769, when Daniel was thirty-four years old and the father of seven children, a lean man rode up to the door of Daniel's cabin, leading several packhorses.

"Would you like to look at some nice goods just brought over from Europe?" the man asked.

Daniel studied him a while. "Be you John Finley?" he asked.

The man's mouth dropped open with surprise. "Be you Dan Boone?" he asked.

The two had not seen or heard of each other since Braddock's defeat, fourteen years before.

4

THE FIRST LOOK

There was great excitement in the Boone cabin that night. Probably Daniel's brother Squire and his brother-in-law John Stuart were there. Daniel's sons James, twelve, and Israel, ten, took part in the conversation and remembered it long afterward. Even his daughters Susannah, eight, and Jemima, seven, stayed up late to listen.

It was a turning point in the life of every one of them, including the three youngest who slept through it. Some historians have said it was a turning point in history, arguing that if Daniel Boone had not led settlers into Kentucky before the Revolution, the British would have retained the land west of the mountains and made it a part of Canada.

John Finley had been in Kentucky again only two years before, trading goods for pelts. The Indians had treated him well, because they profited by his trade, but they watched him closely, so that he did not know whether he was a trader or a prisoner.

He told of a place where salt water flowed from the ground. Buffalo, deer, bear, and many other animals crowded around these salt springs. On the grassy plains buffalo herds were so large that a man might be crushed to death when they stampeded. At the falls on the Ohio River, ducks and wild geese were drawn by the current over the falls and killed, so that a man did not even have to shoot them. He could pick up the dead ones along the banks below the falls.

Finley knew how to get there in a boat on the Ohio River. But the Shawnees, who lived north of the Ohio, watched the river closely. If you wanted to sneak in and do some hunting you would have to go through the mountains. Finley knew there was a gap through the Cumberlands, and from the gap there was a trail called the "Warrior's Path" which led right into the heart of Kentucky.

"If we can find that Cumberland Gap–," he said.

"We can find it," Daniel said. "We go first through the Blue Ridge Mountains, then the Clinch Mountains. I know them like the palm of my hand. Then we come to the Cumberlands, and we can find the gap. We should start right away–this spring–so we'll have good weather."

His two sons, James and Israel, wanted to go. They considered themselves full-grown.

Daniel shook his head. "You will have to stay and help your mother put in the crops. Some of us older men will go and see what the country is like and find some good land, then we'll come back and get the neighbors together. We'll form a big company so we can fight off the Indians, if they object."

"They'll object all right," John Finley predicted.

During the next few weeks, preparations were made. It was decided that Daniel, John Stuart, and John Finley would go, with three hired men as camp keepers, to cook,

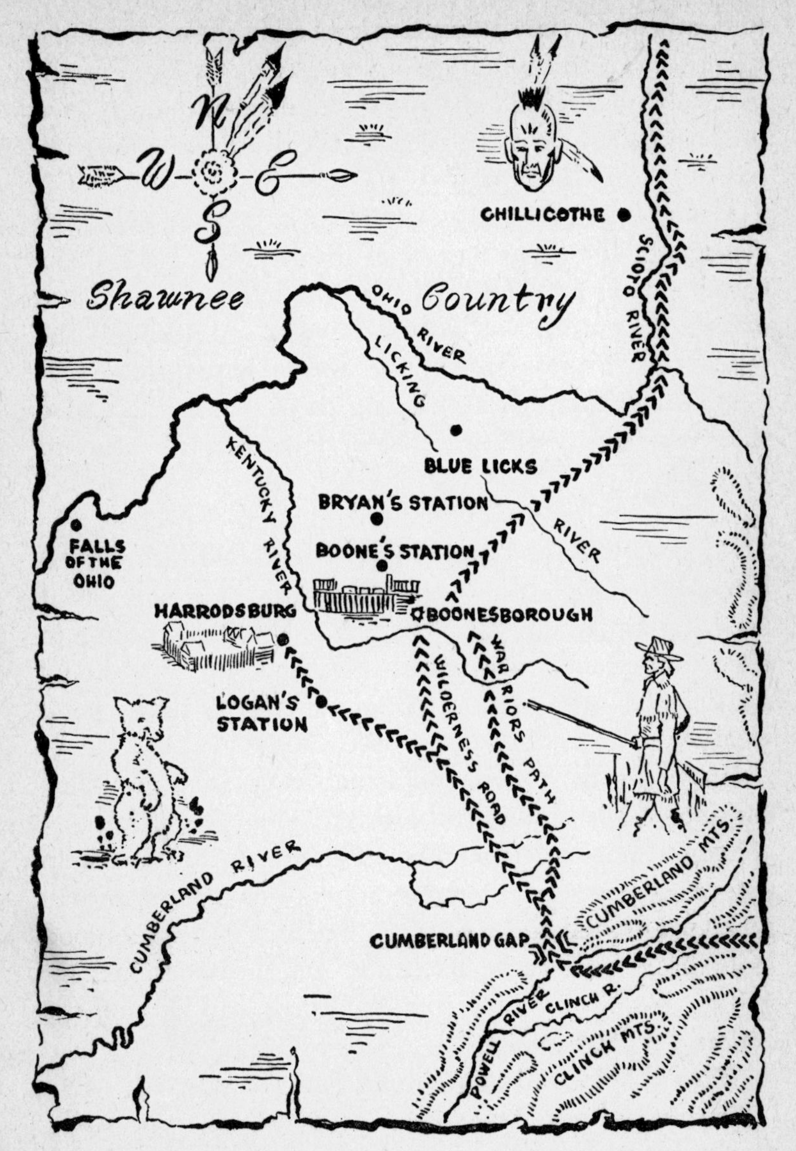

They followed a trail that Finley knew

salt hides and do other chores. Daniel's brother Squire would stay at home and help Daniel's sons put in a crop. Then Squire would go to Kentucky in the late fall, taking a fresh supply of ammunition and other things, and bring back a load of skins and hides to sell.

On May 1, 1769, Daniel Boone, Stuart and Finley started, with three men named Holden, Mooney, and Cooley as camp keepers. All six were mounted, and each led a pack horse carrying bearskin blankets, kettles, salt, extra guns and ammunition, and food for the trip.

They wore loose hunting shirts, trousers, leggings, and moccasins all made of dressed deerskin. Collars of the shirts and seams of the leggings were decorated with fringes. They wore broad leather belts with the buckle in the back so it would not catch in the brush when they crawled. A tomahawk was slung on the right side of the belt. The "shot pouch" filled with lead bullets and the powder horn were attached to a strap that passed over the right shoulder and hung down on the left side.

All the men wore coonskin caps except Daniel. He always wore a felt hat, perhaps because he had worn such a hat as a boy, or perhaps because his skin was tender and he felt more comfortable with a brim over his eyes.

Daniel's deerskin garments were dyed a dull black, and his long hair was braided and tied in two short "clubs" which rested on the back of his neck.

Daniel led the party through the Blue Ridge and Clinch mountains, and here they found a plainly marked trail to Cumberland Gap. Indians had been traveling this trail for centuries.

They traveled slowly, hunting along the way. A cold

rain often drenched them, and they had to stop to dry out their deerskin garments. Daniel saw no signs that Indians had been in the mountains recently.

Near Cumberland Gap they came upon a new cabin. A man named Martin had settled there to trade with the Indians. From his cabin a trail took them to the gap and then northwest through the hills of eastern Kentucky.

On June 7, Finley pointed excitedly at a big hill to the left of the trail.

"That's the hill I've been looking for," he said. "Right on the other side of it are the plains I told you about. Now all we have to do is kill buffalo for a few months, and take the hides back to the settlements and we'll be rich. I had my trading post not far from here. The Indians built some wigwams for the summer and let me keep my goods in one of them."

"Let's camp hereabouts," Daniel said. "Over there on that creek would be a good place for our main station."

He was wrong, as they later learned. They should have built their camp in some hidden place, far from the Warrior's Path. This path, or trail, led from Cumberland Gap northward to the Shawnee country and had been used for centuries by Indians crossing Kentucky.

But they were in too much of a hurry to give the matter much thought. Daniel wanted to have a look at Kentucky. The others wanted to start accumulating a big pile of skins which would make them rich. The three camp keepers started cutting poles for the shelter. Finley and Stuart unloaded the weary pack horses.

Daniel was burning with excitement, although he was outwardly calm as always. Ever since he was a small boy, he had dreamed of this moment, when he could see with his own eyes the rich land west of the mountains. He dismounted, dropped the reins of his horse, and started for the top of the big hill.

This was like the time when he got his job of watching cows in the far pasture. Only now he was not pretending. He was really in the wilds. A few white men had been in Kentucky before him, but they had either hastened through along the river banks or, like Finley, had been prisoners of the Indians and not free to roam.

At the top of the hill he put the butt of his long rifle on the ground, rested his hands on the muzzle and looked. There it was. Level land as far as the eye could reach. Forests and grassy plains. It would take a year or two just to look it over, to get acquainted with the rivers and forests and salt licks, and find a good place to settle.

When he returned to camp, he found that the others had built a big open-faced shelter, with walls on three sides and a steeply pitched roof of interlaced boughs. At the open side, deer meat was roasting over a big bed of coals.

Finley announced that he had done a little exploring in the nearby woods while Daniel was on the hill and had found the site of the temporary village where he had spent the summer. The wigwams had been burned, but some of the posts still stood. Probably there had been a battle there between Cherokees from the south and Shawnees from the north.

No one had yet seen a fresh moccasin track or other Indian sign. After supper the six men spread out their bearskins, lay down under the shelter with their feet toward the dying fire and went to sleep, to dream of hunting.

It is said that the next day, or soon thereafter, Boone, Stuart, and Finley were walking across an open place when they heard a rumble and saw a great herd of buffalo stampeding right toward them.

According to one version of the story, Finley shot the foremost bull and the men huddled behind the big carcass while the herd roared past them. Otherwise, they would have been trampled to death. Another version of the story has it that Boone himself shot the buffalo.

5

DANGERS OF THE WOODS

Game was abundant and it would have been easy to slaughter animals close to the camp and thus quickly build up a store of hides. But the men did not do much hunting close to camp, probably because the stench of decaying flesh would attract flocks of buzzards, and any Indian coming within twenty miles would see the big birds and know what was going on.

The men went out in pairs on long hunts and returned at regular intervals with the hides they had taken. Daniel and Finley went together on the first long hunt, but Finley soon became ill. He was in no danger and needed only to rest a while, so Daniel went on alone to the Kentucky River. Here he saw rich land where corn would grow well, good timber for cabin logs, and springs of pure water. Here, he decided, he would build a settlement.

For nearly six months the men hunted and explored, and no one saw Indian signs. When the main camp was well stocked with hides, they built outlying camps and stored hides in them.

While the others dreamed of the luxuries they would enjoy when they got back to the settlements, Daniel thought of wagons loaded with supplies, of axes to cut a road through the wilderness, of the cabin he would build on the Kentucky River for Rebecca and the children.

In low places along the banks of rivers and creeks were canebrakes, some of them covering hundreds of acres. The cane stalks were ten to thirty feet high. Buffalo wintered in the canebrakes, making trails as broad as a street.

Late in December, Daniel, John Stuart, and one of the camp keepers were living at an outlying camp near a big canebrake. One morning Daniel and Stuart went into the brake to hunt buffalo.

As they were walking along a "buffalo street," they came face to face with a party of mounted Shawnees, painted red and black for war. There was no use resisting or trying to escape.

"Pretend you're glad to see them," Boone said quickly to Stuart. "If we expect them to treat us well they probably will." He smiled and called "How d' do," to the Indians.

A big warrior rode up to them, dismounted, and took their rifles. "How d' do," he said.

This was Daniel's first contact with the Shawnees, and he did not know their language. But he knew some of the sign language by which Indians of different tribes talked to each other. The big warrior knew a few words of English.

By signs, gestures, and words the big Indian ordered them to take him to their camp. Daniel quickly agreed.

As they approached the outlying camp, Daniel talked loudly to the Indians. The camp keeper saw them coming and ducked into the woods.

The Indians saw at a glance that this was not the main

camp, because no ammunition and only a few supplies were stored there. They loaded the little stock of hides on their horses and ordered Daniel to take them to the big camp.

He pretended not to understand and cheerfully led them to another small camp. He wanted to give the camp keeper plenty of time to warn the men at the main camp. He was sure that these men would load their big stack of hides on the pack horses and get out of sight.

The Indians again ordered him to take them to the big camp. Again he misunderstood. But when all the outlying camps had been visited, he took them at last to the big one. To his dismay, the hides, the pack horses, and supplies were still there. Finley and the three camp keepers had simply hidden in the woods.

The Indians were delighted. Quickly they loaded this fortune on the pack horses and started north, taking Daniel and Stuart with them. Evidently they did not suspect that four other white men were hiding thereabouts.

The big Indian who commanded the Shawnees was known as Captain Will, probably because his Indian name sounded something like Will. At any rate Daniel and Stuart called him Captain Will.

The Indians were not in a bad mood, particularly after getting all this loot. They did not want scalps of white men because they were then at peace with the whites. But Captain Will made it plain that the whites had no right to hunt in Kentucky. Buffalo, deer, and bear were the cattle of the Shawnees. The white men were cattle thieves, in Captain Will's opinion.

"What do you think they'll do with us?" Stuart asked

Daniel as the two were marching along with their hands bound.

"That depends on the way we act," Daniel said. "Indians, I think, are like whites. If you think they are going to hurt you and show it, they will probably hurt you. Even dumb brutes are like that. If you are afraid of a dog, he knows it, and he gets worried and bites you."

Going on this theory, Daniel and Stuart laughed often and pretended they did not have a worry in the world. Actually they were bitter and discouraged. They had spent all their savings on this trip. They had worked hard for six months to get their hides. They had dreamed great dreams. Now everything was swept away.

A few days later, as they were approaching the Ohio River, Captain Will turned them loose.

"Now, brothers, go home and stay there," he said. "This is Shawnee land, and the Long Knives cannot hunt here. If you come here again, wasps and yellow jackets will sting you."

He said this not as it is written here, but by signs and gestures. Indians called white men "Long Knives," probably because white hunters carried long hunting knives.

Captain Will gave them moccasins, a short-barreled gun, and enough powder and shot to kill game for themselves on the way home. He shook hands with them and said good-bye.

Daniel and Stuart were in no mood to go home. They felt they had been robbed and insulted, and Captain Will's little joke about yellow jackets aroused their cold fury. As soon as they were out of sight of the Indians, they turned and followed.

That night they crept up on the Indians, caught four horses and rode south.

At daybreak they paused to let the horses graze and lay down for a rest. An hour later, Captain Will and his warriors galloped up.

Looking into the muzzles of a half-dozen rifles, Daniel knew that his life was over if he showed the slightest fear or anger. "How d' do!" he called, in glad surprise. He laughed as if he had played a wonderful trick.

Captain Will glared at him and lowered his rifle. It is hard to shoot a man who is laughing. Captain Will dismounted. "Steal horses," he said.

He walked up to Daniel and put a bell on his neck. Then he ordered Daniel to gallop around the clearing, like a horse which has been turned out to graze. The warriors roared with laughter.

When this entertainment was over, the Indians started north again with their captives. Captain Will said he would not turn them loose this time until they were north of the Ohio River.

At dusk, when the Indians were preparing to camp for the night, Daniel and Stuart dashed into a canebrake. The Indians took after them with whoops. But it is very hard to find a man in a canebrake. After a long search, the Indians gave up and went to sleep.

A few days later, Boone and Stuart arrived, tired and hungry, at their main camp. Finley and the three camp keepers had started home, but Boone and Stuart soon overtook them. A gloomy conference was held beside the Warrior's Path. It was a "time of sorrow," as Daniel said later. They had lost everything except a few rifles and a little store of ammunition.

Finley and the camp keepers had seen enough of Kentucky. It was no place for them, they said.

Boone and Stuart argued that Kentucky was not to blame. They shouldn't have built a camp close to the Warrior's Path. Next time they would know better. There was still a fortune all around them.

While they were talking, they heard or saw someone approaching. Daniel grabbed a rifle and stood behind a tree trunk. The others got out of sight in the bushes.

Daniel saw two men riding toward him, but he could not tell whether they were whites or Indians.

"Hello, strangers! Who are you?" he called.

"White men and friends," came the reply.

It was Daniel's younger brother, Squire, and a man named Alexander Neeley. They had brought a good supply of rifles, ammunition, traps, and other equipment and were eager to get rich.

Finley and the three camp keepers could not be persuaded to stay and the next day they started for home. Nobody knows what became of them. A few years later a man named John Finley was robbed by the Indians in Pennsylvania. Maybe it was the same Finley.

Daniel and Squire Boone, Stuart, and Neeley established a new camp near the junction of the Red and Kentucky rivers, far from the Warrior's Path, and set out traps for beaver and otter. Each man had his own string of traps and went out alone to gather the pelts. They met at the camp every two weeks.

At one of these meetings Stuart did not appear, and Daniel went out to look for him. He found only the ashes of a campfire and Stuart's initials carved on a tree.

Stuart's disappearance frightened Neeley. For the first

time he realized how dangerous it was to live in the Kentucky woods. He began to imagine brown-skinned warriors in every bush and to hear them creeping up on him at night. Finally he admitted that he could not stand it any longer and saddled his horse and rode away.

Daniel continued to search for Stuart but at last gave up hope. "I loved the man like a brother," he said. The two had hunted together for years.

Daniel and Squire Boone became more cautious. They kept together. They built a fire only at night, when the smoke could not be seen, and in a sheltered place so the flames could not be seen. Whenever possible they walked in streams, where the current would wash away their tracks or on hard rock or along the trunks of fallen trees. Close to camp they scattered dry leaves over their tracks. Once they saw the print of Indian moccasins near their camp site and quickly moved to another place.

In May, 1770, their ammunition was running low. Squire loaded their pelts on the horses and left for the Yadkin Valley, promising to return late in July. Daniel remained alone, without a horse or dog to keep him company.

He had enough ammunition to kill food for himself but not enough to lay up a stock of hides. There was nothing to do but explore, which is exactly what he wanted to do. He went westward along the Ohio to the falls, where Louisville is now located, then returned through central Kentucky. In later years someone asked him if he was ever lost in the wilderness. "I can't say as ever I was lost," he replied, "but I was bewildered once for three days."

One day on this return trip he discovered that Indians were following him. He tried to elude them, but there was no good cover. He ran and they took after him with whoops.

He came to the edge of a bluff and looked down. There was a sheer drop of some fifty feet and no possibility of climbing down. He was trapped.

Far beneath him was the top of a sugar-maple tree. He backed off a few paces and took a running broad jump into space.

He hurtled down into the top of the tree. The limbs bent under his weight and let him gently down to the ground. He ducked into the bushes and looked up. The Indians were leaning over the edge of the cliff and talking in excited tones. It seemed to them that the white man had flown away like a bird.

Daniel hurtled down into the top of the tree

6

DEATH ON THE TRAIL

Daniel Boone now knew more about Kentucky than did any other white man. He knew its woods and plains, its streams, hills, and caves, its animals, birds, and plants.

From his experiences with Captain Will's band, he knew that the wild Shawnees living north of the Ohio were neither bloody monsters nor fools, but people. They would fight for Kentucky, as the whites would fight if a horde of Indians swarmed into North Carolina and took the best farms.

But there was no point in hating or despising Indians just because their skin was a different color. That sort of hatred led to bloodshed and needless massacres of both whites and Indians. When stupid, hot-tempered white men killed friendly Indians, or killed prisoners taken in battle, or scalped fallen Indians, other whites had to suffer for it.

Later, in his many battles with Indians, Daniel Boone never took a scalp or permitted his men to mistreat prisoners. He deceived the Indians whenever he could, for deception is a part of war, but he never cheated them. And he built a reputation among the Indians which saved his life on many occasions.

Squire Boone returned to Kentucky as he had promised, and on July 27 the two brothers met at the appointed place. Squire reported that Daniel's wife and children were well and fairly prosperous. Squire had sold the beaver and otter pelts at a good price and paid off his own and Daniel's debts.

Squire Boone had now traveled the long and dangerous trail from the Yadkin Valley to Kentucky three times with a string of pack horses. Fortunately he had not encountered any Indians, but his success was not due to luck alone. As a hunter, explorer, and later as an Indian fighter, he displayed ability and courage equal to that of his famous brother.

With the ammunition Squire had brought, the two brothers set about the hard task of accumulating another load of hides. Sometimes they lived in caves, but usually they camped in the thick woods. Once a wolf sneaked up to their camp in the gray dawn and carried off Daniel's hat. Daniel was outraged by this theft. He had to have a hat. He trailed the wolf, shot it, and recovered his hat, somewhat chewed but still wearable.

In the fall Squire took another load of hides east. He was supposed to return immediately but was delayed, and Daniel started east to meet him. On the Warrior's Path Daniel came upon an old Indian who had collapsed from hunger and weariness. Daniel killed a deer and fed the old man.

Soon after that he met Squire and the two returned for another winter of trapping. In the spring of 1771 they both started east with a valuable load of pelts. When they were almost home they met a party of Indians who robbed them of their furs, rifles, ammunition, and horses.

They reached home poorer than they had been when they began their Kentucky adventure two years before.

But Daniel did not consider the time wasted. He had learned a great deal, and he was convinced that Kentucky could be settled. He knew what he wanted to do with his life.

Moreover, he discovered that he was famous. People far and near had heard of his exploits and came to him with questions. "Can we go there now? Is it safe? Is the land good?"

For two years Daniel talked about Kentucky, and people listened. Early in 1773 he and a few other men made a brief visit to Kentucky to look at the land. When they returned, Daniel heard reports that parties of settlers were preparing to move there.

Feeling there was no time to lose, Daniel sold his farm and bought horses, cattle, pigs, rifles, ammunition, and other supplies.

In September, 1773, Daniel, Squire, and about a dozen other Yadkin Valley farmers and their wives and children, numbering forty persons in all, mounted horses and started for Kentucky. They could not take wagons because the trail was so narrow at some places that a loaded pack horse could hardly squeeze through.

Probably the youngest of these pioneers was Daniel's son John, only a few months old. Rebecca must have carried him in her arms.

Daniel, Squire and a few other men rode ahead, finding the trail and watching for Indian signs. Women and children followed, riding gentle and dependable horses. Behind the women and children were pack horses loaded with supplies. Finally came the cattle and pigs, driven by men and half-grown boys. It is no easy task to drive cattle and pigs along a narrow mountain trail. They have their own ideas. One man who made this trip later wrote, "Who ever drives cattle here ought to have patience in great abundance."

There was no sign of Indians, and the frontier had been quiet for some time, so no one feared an attack. At night they did not even put out sentries. They were all so weary that they felt they were more likely to die of fatigue than of Indian bullets. Besides, they had plenty of dogs with them. "If Indians come, the dogs will bark," they said.

In Powell's Valley, near Cumberland Gap, they passed a trading post owned by a Captain William Russell. A few miles beyond the post, some of the families discovered they were running out of flour. Daniel's oldest son, James, volunteered to go back to the post and buy flour. Daniel agreed.

James was sixteen years old and large and strong. He was a good hunter and woodsman, and for years he had been doing a man's work on the farm. Except for Squire, he was probably the most capable man that Daniel had in his little force of riflemen.

James rode back to Russell's post and purchased the flour. Russell's son, about seventeen, two white men who worked for Russell, and two Negro slaves belonging to Russell, started out with James to help him transport the flour.

When night came, they camped about three miles behind the main party.

At dawn a party of Indians fired into the camp. James Boone and the Russell boy were so badly wounded that they could not stand. One of the white workmen and one Negro were killed. The other white workman was badly wounded but ran into the woods, where he died. The other Negro was not hurt and witnessed what followed from a hiding place in the woods.

These Indians were no better than some whites who raided Indian villages and scalped women and children. While James Boone and the Russell boy pleaded for mercy, the Indians tortured them to death.

Captain Russell, owner of the trading post, and some other men arrived at the scene of the murders soon after the Indians had departed. One of them hurried forward to warn Boone's party while the others buried the bodies.

When Daniel heard what had happened, he quickly got his people into a ravine and posted sentries. Rebecca sent a linen sheet back to cover the body of her son.

The Indians attacked the people in the ravine but were driven off. It is said that Daniel killed one of them.

While Daniel and Rebecca mourned their son, others in the group became panic-stricken. Cattle and horses had scattered through the woods, and many could not be found after the battle.

Sadly and fearfully the little party turned back. Most of them returned to their former homes in the Yadkin Valley. But Daniel and Rebecca had sold their farm and had no place to go.

There was a small fort near Cumberland Gap, called Snoddy's. Here Daniel and his family lived through the winter. Daniel and his fourteen-year-old son Israel hunted to provide for the others.

In May, 1774, Daniel rode alone back to Powell's Valley to visit his son's grave. He found that the wolves had started digging at the graves. He dug down and made sure that the bodies had not been disturbed. Then he refilled the graves and piled logs and stones on them to keep the wolves away.

As he finished the work, a violent storm came up. The rain was so heavy that he could not see to travel. He sat down on a log and waited while the storm howled around him. The almost unbearable grief over losing James and the memory of his many failures brought upon him a fit of melancholy unlike anything he had ever experienced before. Years later he said this was the worst moment of his life.

After the storm abated, he moved some distance from the graves, put a hobble on his horse, that is, tied its front feet together so it would not wander far, and lay down for the night. He could not sleep.

Daniel crawled away through the wet bushes

The sky cleared, but his mental agony continued. He felt that his life was worthless.

Suddenly he heard stealthy noises in the bushes. Indians were creeping up on him.

As quietly as possible he crawled away through the wet bushes. In the distance he heard the little bell ringing which he had tied to his horse's neck. Slowly he made his way toward this sound, caught his horse, and mounted. He did not know how many Indians were hunting him or where they were, so he could not ride directly toward the trail.

He urged the horse forward slowly, tinkling the bell from time to time so the Indians would think the horse was still grazing. When he had ridden some distance this way, he silenced the bell and galloped off.

7

BOONESBOROUGH IS BUILT

The murder of James Boone and his companions in Powell's Valley was only one of many brutal acts that aroused anger on the frontier that winter. In western Virginia, a party of white men invited several Indians to their camp for a feast and murdered them without provocation. In North Carolina a group of peaceful Cherokees came to a white settlement to watch a horse race. A white man stabbed one of them to death just because he hated Indians. He was not punished.

In the spring of 1774, about the time Daniel was visiting his son's grave, a man named James Harrod took thirty-four riflemen into Kentucky and began building log cabins near the Kentucky River. The Shawnee Indians north of the Ohio heard of this and began preparing for war.

The governor of Virginia knew that trouble was coming and sent a message to Captain William Russell who kept the trading post in Powell's Valley. The message instructed Russell to select two "faithful woodsmen" to go into Kentucky and warn Harrod of his danger. Russell selected Daniel Boone and a big Pennsylvania German named Mike Stoner for this dangerous mission.

Daniel and Mike made a quick trip into Kentucky and warned Harrod. Daniel had recovered from his bleak despair and was once again enthusiastic about living in Kentucky. He remained long enough in the new settlement, called Harrodsburg, to build a cabin for himself. He hoped to return soon with his family.

Daniel and Mike then turned north to warn other men who were believed to be surveying land near the Ohio River. One amusing incident of this trip has been remembered.

In northeastern Kentucky there are rich deposits of salt just beneath the surface. Salt water flows from hillsides at various places. For hundreds of thousands of years animals came here to lick salt. A stream which flows through this region is called the Licking River because there are so many salt licks along its banks.

At one place, called Blue Licks, buffalo, over thousands of years, had licked out broad trenches eight or ten feet deep.

When Daniel and Mike came to Blue Licks, they saw a big buffalo bull licking busily in one of these trenches. Another trench ran close to it, so that only a thin wall of earth separated the two, and there was a hole in the wall.

"Let's have some fun," said Mike.

He crawled into the second trench, took off his cap and thrust it through the hole right into the bull's face. Mike expected the bull to be very frightened, but he did not know the breed very well. The bull lowered his head and charged through the wall.

Mike scrambled out of the trench shouting "Shoot him, Captain! Shoot him, Captain!"

Seeing that Mike was in no danger, Daniel doubled up on the ground and rolled with laughter.

Daniel and Mike found at least some of the men they were looking for and warned them to leave. These men thanked them and left. Harrod and his party also departed, leaving their cabins unprotected. Daniel and Mike returned to North Carolina in August.

That fall Indians and whites were at war along the Virginia and North Carolina borders. Daniel Boone joined the militia, fought in a few skirmishes and was promoted to captain. In October a force of militia defeated a Shawnee army on the Virginia frontier and peace was restored. Daniel made plans for another attempt to settle in Kentucky.

On March 10, 1775, he started for Kentucky with a force of about thirty men, including his brother Squire, his big friend Mike Stoner, and a neighbor named Richard Callaway. They were all mounted and led a few pack horses, but they did not attempt to take livestock. They were traveling light.

On the first day they killed a bear and had a fine supper. As one of the men later wrote, "every heart abounded with joy and excitement in anticipating the new things we should see and the romantic scenes through which we must pass." Not expecting trouble from the Indians, they did not post sentries at night.

After passing through Cumberland Gap they left the Warrior's Path and began cutting a road through the wilderness toward the place on the Kentucky River which Daniel had selected long before. They called it the Wilderness Road.

One day, as they were working on this road, one of

the men called out in surprise. He had found a skeleton in a hollow tree. Daniel investigated. Beside the skeleton was a powder horn with the initials *J.S.*

"That's John Stuart's powder horn," he said. "I loved the man like a brother. He disappeared hereabouts five years ago."

They searched the surrounding woods but found no rifle or other equipment. One arm of the skeleton was broken and the bone still had the mark of a lead bullet on it. There were no marks of a scalping knife on the skull.

Evidently Stuart had been wounded by the Indians and had hidden in the tree and died from loss of blood.

On March 23 the men camped in the woods some fifteen miles from their destination. At dawn the next morning they were awakened by a volley of rifle fire. There was great confusion. Some ran half-naked into the woods. Daniel grabbed a rifle and rallied the men. Indians charged them but were driven off. Two men had been killed and one badly wounded by the first volley.

Some of the men were so badly frightened by this attack that they mounted their horses and departed for North Carolina. Daniel and the rest resumed their journey as soon as the wounded man was able to travel.

When they came to the Kentucky River, they saw a cheerful sight. Several hundred buffalo were moving across a grassy plain, "some running, some walking, others loping slowly and carelessly, with young calves playing, skipping and bounding through the plain." They would have plenty of meat in this new land.

Where Otter Creek flows into the Kentucky River they started building a settlement which they named Boonesborough. Thirty miles to the west were the cabins which James Harrod had built the summer before. For some reason the Indians had not burned these cabins. Harrod and his men were now back building more cabins.

Soon other bands of men rode into Kentucky. Some remained at Boonesborough, while others established settlements of their own. Kentucky was booming.

In May, delegates from the various settlements met under a huge elm tree and established a government for the territory, then called Transylvania. Daniel Boone, Squire Boone, and Colonel Richard Callaway represented Boonesborough. Daniel introduced a bill in this new legislature "for improving the breed of horses," and the bill was quickly passed. From that day to this, Kentucky people have been greatly interested in horses.

At Boonesborough, as at other new settlements, the cabins were built around a large rectangle, facing into the center. The plan was to build a heavy log wall from one cabin to the next, so that when the structure was completed the walls and the cabins would form a stockade, with a gate in each of two sides.

At a time of danger, the livestock could be kept inside the stockade. Riflemen could fire over the walls to drive off the Indians.

When a number of cabins had been built and work was started on the log wall, Daniel, Squire, Colonel Callaway, and others went east to get their families.

Early in September Daniel returned with Rebecca, his son Israel, now sixteen, his daughter Jemima, thirteen, and four younger children. One of his daughters was already married and remained in the Yadkin Valley.

"We arrived safe," Daniel later said, "my wife and

daughter being the first white women that ever stood on the banks of the Kentucky River."

There is no record of what Rebecca thought when she first saw the little line of cabins. The stockade had not been finished. If a party of Indians had attacked at that time they could have walked right into the settlement. Winter was coming soon, food was scarce, and the supply of ammunition was running low.

Of the five hundred people who came to Kentucky that summer, three hundred lost their nerve and returned east. The troubles of Boonesborough and Harrodsburg were only beginning.

In December a little party of Indians crept up on Boonesborough and captured two boys. Daniel Boone led a party of men in pursuit of the Indians. They found the body of one boy. No one knows what became of the other.

Meanwhile astonishing news came from the east. New England farmers and villagers had defeated British troops at Concord and Lexington and had killed many redcoats on Bunker Hill. A man from Virginia, named George Washington, had been appointed commander of the colonial forces.

"I know of him," Daniel said. "He was with Braddock's army and was about the only officer with any sense. That's when I had to cut the traces and ride fast to get away from the Indians."

8

ADVENTURE OF THREE GIRLS

Now that the thirteen colonies were in full revolt against the rule of King George, the British reasoned that if they could persuade the Shawnees to attack the new settlements in Kentucky, General George Washington would have to send part of his army west to defend Kentucky.

British agents went to the Shawnees, who lived north of Kentucky, and made a proposition. "If you will fight the Long Knives in Kentucky," they said, "we will give you guns and ammunition and much red paint, so your braves can paint their faces for war. The whites are taking your best hunting grounds. You can drive them out."

Chief Cornstalk, Chief Blackfish, and other great Shawnee chiefs listened to these British agents and agreed to think the matter over.

Probably other British agents went to the Cherokees, who lived south of Kentucky, with a similar proposition, urging them to forget their ancient differences with the Shawnees and help the Shawnees fight the Kentucky settlers. At any rate there was much war talk among young Cherokee braves, so the Cherokees selected one of their chiefs, Hanging Maw, to go north and discuss the matter with the Shawnees.

Hanging Maw got his name because he had a habit of letting his big mouth hang open. But despite his funny appearance, he was a shrewd man and a good diplomat. With two other warriors he slipped into Kentucky, and there he met, by accident, two Shawnee hunters who agreed to lead him north to the Shawnee land.

On the afternoon of Sunday, July 7, 1776, the five crept into a canebrake across the river from Boonesborough to see what they could see.

That same afternoon, Daniel Boone was resting in his cabin. Because he had been to meeting that morning, he was not dressed in his usual buckskin garments but wore his best pantaloons. They were made of homespun cloth, but for the frontier they were quite elegant.

He took off his coat and hung it on a peg, removed his shoes and shoved them under the bed where the children would not stumble over them. He pulled off his stockings and stretched out for a nap.

His daughter Jemima, now fourteen, was visiting at the Callaway cabin with her friends Betsey, sixteen, and Fanny, fourteen. All three girls wore their Sunday-go-to-meeting dresses, with long skirts which came to their ankles. Betsey, because she was grown-up, wore shoes. Grown women of Boonesborough wore shoes on Sunday but went barefooted during the week. Jemima Boone and Fanny Callaway, not quite grown-up, still did not have Sunday shoes and so were barefooted.

Betsey Callaway wanted to go for a walk, but Jemima Boone did not feel at her best striding along barefooted beside the queenly Betsey in shoes. Moreover, Jemima had stepped on a cane stub that morning and hurt her heel, so she had to tiptoe on one foot.

"Let's go for a canoe ride," she said.

She felt she would look well sitting in a canoe. Fanny also voted for a canoe ride. So the three went down to the river bank, climbed into Daniel's birchbark canoe, and shoved off.

They had much to talk about—namely, three young men. Betsey was soon to be married to handsome Samuel Henderson. Fanny had her eye on John Holder. Jemima Boone was in love with Flanders Callaway, a cousin of Betsey and Fanny. But Jemima was unhappy because her father did not approve of Flanders. Daniel considered Flanders a callow youth and said that he and Jemima were too young to get married.

This seemed very unjust to Jemima. Flanders was eighteen. Men of that age often married girls of fourteen.

So, as the canoe drifted down the river, Betsey talked about Samuel, Fanny about John, and Jemima about Flanders. Jemima put her leg over the side of the canoe and dangled her sore foot in the water. Of course, if Flanders happened to stroll past on the bank, she would pull in her foot and look grown-up.

"Let's paddle over to the other shore and pick some flowers," Betsey suggested.

"No," Jemima said. "I'm afraid of Indians."

The others laughed. They knew she was pretending. For months there had been no sign of Indians.

"You want to stay in the canoe because you hope Flanders will walk past and see you," Betsey said.

The three girls talked for a long time until they noticed that the current had carried them far down the stream and close to the opposite shore. Then they turned the canoe about, to paddle back, and got stuck on a sand bar. They put their paddles down and tried to shove off, but the back end of the canoe swung around close to the canebrake.

It was just at this spot that Hanging Maw and his four companions had hidden in order to spy on Boonesborough.

A brown arm reached out and grabbed the canoe. The girls screamed, but they were too far from the settlement to be heard. The five warriors waded into the shallow water and seized them. Fanny struck one warrior with her paddle so hard that the paddle broke, but he was not hurt at all. He grabbed Betsey by the hair and flourished his knife. This meant that he would scalp her if she did not keep quiet. The girls quit screaming.

The braves lifted them from the boat and carried them across a hill, out of sight of the river. Hanging Maw knew some English. "Your name?" he asked Jemima.

"Jemima Boone," she said proudly.

"Boone!" Hanging Maw exclaimed. Every Cherokee knew of the great hunter, Daniel Boone.

"Your sisters?" he asked, pointing to the Callaway girls.

"Yes," Jemima lied. She believed the other girls would get better treatment if the Indians thought they were also daughters of her father.

Jemima knew a great deal about Indian ways from what her father and others had told her. She guessed that these warriors did not intend to kill them but would take them away as captives. Their only hope was to delay the Indians as much as possible and leave a plain trail for Boonesborough men to follow. Mumbling and talking rapidly, so that Hanging Maw could not understand, she conveyed her plan to the other girls.

Her foot suddenly became so sore that she could hardly step on it. She stopped and complained. An Indian shoved her and she fell down, probably digging her fingers into the earth, so her father would see these handprints. She arose with dignity and said she would not go another step. She signaled to Betsey to dig her shoe heels into the ground whenever possible. Now Fanny's feet also became tender.

Beneath his war paint, Hanging Maw had a kind heart, and he was especially fond of children. These white squaws were hardly more than children and he felt sorry for them. He dug into a supply pack and took out two pair of moccasins, the smallest he could find, and gave them to the barefooted girls. With his scalping knife he cut the girls' skirts off at the knees so they could walk more easily. Then he helped them bind the cloth around their bare legs as protection against brambles.

He was quite pleased with himself. The Shawnees would be impressed when he turned over to them three daughters of Daniel Boone, chief of the Long Knives.

After this considerable delay, the little party started north. Jemima stumbled, clutched a bush, and fell down. She got up and staggered on, but she had broken a little branch on that bush. In a short time the leaves of the broken branch would begin to wither, and Daniel Boone would know they had passed this way.

While Jemima was creating a disturbance and the Indians were watching her, Betsey would drop a bit of cloth on the ground. She tore up her handkerchief and dropped a corner on which the name Callaway was embroidered.

After covering some ten or twelve miles, the Indians

An Indian shoved her

camped for the night. They gave the girls smoked buffalo tongue for supper. This was a great delicacy on the frontier. Then they bound each girl's elbows together behind her back with a thong and set her against a tree. One end of the thong was tied around the tree and the other around the wrist of a warrior. Thus the girls had to sit up all night leaning against a tree, while the warriors slept comfortably.

At daybreak the march began again, and soon they came upon a stray pony in the woods. Hanging Maw caught the pony and put the girls on it. This way he hoped to make better time. He started off, leading the pony.

There was a scream. Jemima fell off.

Hanging Maw laughed. "White squaw no good," he said. "Can't ride horse."

Patiently he put Jemima back. She fell off again, dragging the other girls with her.

Now Hanging Maw himself mounted the pony and showed them how to ride. It was no use. As soon as the march resumed, one of the girls, or all three, got overbalanced and tumbled to the ground. Even the pony got disgusted with such awkwardness and bit Betsey's arm. Finally, the Indians decided that white squaws just could not learn to ride, so they turned the pony loose and forced the girls to walk.

About noon they came to a canebrake. The Indians stopped and talked for a few minutes, then Hanging Maw told Betsey to take off her shoes. Fearfully, she obeyed. Hanging Maw pried the heels off of them and handed them back to her. As they resumed the march, Hanging Maw told the girls not to drop any more twigs or pieces of cloth.

Meanwhile there was great excitement at Boonesborough. Before Daniel finished his Sunday nap, someone saw the empty canoe on the other shore and shouted the alarm. Daniel leaped up, grabbed his rifle and ran out barefooted. Young Samuel Henderson, the one who was engaged to marry Betsey, had just finished shaving one side of his face when the alarm came. He rushed out, leaving half his face unshaven.

Daniel and other men crossed the river and soon found the trail. They easily guessed what had happened. Colonel Callaway, father of Betsey and Fanny, suggested that a party of men should follow on horseback and overtake the Indians as soon as possible. Daniel pointed out that the Indians would hear horsemen approaching and might tomahawk the girls. This had happened to a woman captive at another settlement. He said they must follow afoot and try to take the Indians by surprise.

He started out, studying the ground, and the others followed. They were all dressed in their Sunday clothes, which were not suitable for a job like this. Daniel was still barefooted.

When night came and they could no longer see the trail, they lay down to rest. One man went back to Boonesborough and returned with a pack of buckskin clothes and moccasins, ammunition, and jerked venison.

At dawn they started again, finding broken branches, heel prints, and bits of cloth. The trail was plain. Either the Indians did not care if they were followed, or they wanted to be followed. Daniel told his men to watch for an ambush.

Certainly Daniel was suffering agonies of fear for the safety of his daughter, but outwardly he was perfectly calm. This was characteristic. When other men were shaking with fright, boiling with anger, or sunk in despair, he was thinking and acting.

Alternately running and walking through open places, creeping stealthily toward ravines where warriors might be hidden, Daniel led his men along the trail until the middle of the afternoon. Then he stopped. The trail ended abruptly at a stream.

The men examined every inch of ground on a dozen buffalo streets leading from the canebrake on the bank of the stream but found nothing. Daniel Boone stood, leaning on his tall rifle, thinking. He was remembering the lay of the land in northern Kentucky, and considering the ways of Indians.

Samuel Henderson, John Holder, and Flanders Callaway, sweethearts of the kidnaped girls, were with the trailing party, and they were in despair. They knew it would take hours, perhaps the rest of the day, to find the trail in the woods or canebrake. The men would have to search the ground for many miles over a wide area. Already the Indians were far ahead. There seemed no hope of overtaking them before they reached the Ohio. If the girls were taken across the Ohio, not even an army could rescue them.

Suddenly Daniel called to the men. "Never mind the trail," he said. "They don't want us to follow any farther, and that means they're not planning an ambush but they're heading for the Shawnee camps on the Scioto River. I know how they'll go."

He set off at such a rapid pace that only the most athletic of the men could keep up.

Once he turned to young Flanders Callaway, Jemima's

friend, who was right at his heels, and said, "You're coming along very well." Flanders was greatly pleased.

At night the men flung themselves down for a few hours of sleep, and at dawn they started again. Daniel stopped on the bank of a small stream. "They crossed hereabouts," he said. "Look for tracks."

They followed the stream and within two hundred yards they found fresh tracks. The water was still muddy.

An hour later they found the carcass of a buffalo which had been killed that morning.

"At the next watering place, they'll stop to cook the meat they cut from this carcass," Daniel said.

Now the men crept forward with great caution. One of them found a snake which the Indians had killed. It was still wriggling.

About noon they came to a stream, and Daniel gave his orders in a whisper. "Some of you go downstream with Henderson, and cross and circle back. The rest come with me. They're not far away. We'll surround them."

Meanwhile the three girls were waiting for dinner in a clump of trees on the other side of the stream and had no idea that help was near. Betsey Callaway was sitting on the ground, and Jemima and Fanny were lying with their heads in her lap.

They were now more than thirty miles from Boonesborough. The Indians had confused the trail in many places by following buffalo trails where footprints would not show and by wading in streams.

The girls could tell that the Indians themselves no longer feared pursuit, and they knew that if an Indian feels safe in the woods, he probably is safe.

One Indian had been posted as a sentry on a hill. Another built a fire. A third lazily put buffalo meat on a stick for roasting. Hanging Maw went down to the stream to fill a kettle.

The sentry was so sure that no whites were about that he leaned his rifle against a tree and came down to the fire to light his pipe.

Jemima was wearily watching the warrior put meat on the stick, when suddenly a spurt of blood seemed to come from the brown skin on his shoulder and a shot rang out.

"That's Daddy," she screamed, jumping up.

"Run, gals!" someone called to them. The girls ran.

"That's Daddy," she screamed

The Indian hit in the shoulder fell into the fire but leaped up and sprinted for a canebrake nearby without waiting to pick up his rifle.

The sentry hurled a tomahawk past Betsey's head as she ran.

"Fall down!" came a command.

The girls recognized Daniel's voice and fell to the ground. Guns blazed all around.

The other Indians now ran for the canebrake as Daniel and his men charged toward the fire.

Betsey Callaway stood up from a clump of bushes. With her deeply tanned skin and black hair she looked like an Indian. One of the men raised his empty rifle to strike her with the butt. Daniel grabbed his arm.

"Don't kill her now," he said calmly, "when we traveled so far to save her."

In their disorderly retreat to the canebrake, none of the Indians had taken time to grab up a rifle, so the whites did not fear an attack. There was no use looking for an Indian in a canebrake, so the whites sat down and ate the meat which the Indians had left.

Next morning the party started home. On the way they caught the stray pony, and now the girls could ride very well. Even Jemima's sore foot had healed overnight.

As soon as they reached Boonesborough, Samuel Henderson shaved both sides of his face. Within a month he and Betsey were married. There was "dancing to fiddle music by the light of tallow dips, and a treat of home-grown watermelons of which the whole station was proud."

Daniel and Jemima had a private talk. "I was wrong about Flanders Callaway," Daniel admitted. "He's a real man."

When Jemima married Flanders and Fanny married John Holder, the watermelon season was past, but there was again much dancing to fiddle music.

There was one other great celebration that year. A traveler arrived with a newspaper only a few months old. The Boonesborough citizens gathered, and someone read aloud the Declaration of Independence. The thirteen colonies, and Kentucky, were now free and independent.

The settlers built a bonfire. The fiddler tuned up, and there was more dancing. Never again would the British King tell them what to do.

History tells us that Hanging Maw got back to the Cherokee country safely and lived to a ripe old age, finally becoming a good friend of the whites.

9

BLOOD FREEZES ON A BLADE

On New Year's Day, 1777, a little procession of exhausted men and women and frightened children halted at Boonesborough. They were from McClelland's station, a settlement farther north. For two days they had defended their stockade against a strong force of Indians, but they knew they could not withstand another such attack. They were going east to safety.

Ten Boonesborough men went with them. They too had seen too much of the dark and bloody ground. Only thirty riflemen now remained at Boonesborough.

From Harrodsburg came word that Indians had killed two men. Other settlements reported that several of their hunters had been killed near the Licking River. Worry grew into panic. Most of the newer settlements were abandoned, leaving only Boonesborough, Harrodsburg, and Logan's Station still occupied. Logan's was about twenty miles south of Harrodsburg.

At Boonesborough, men, women and children worked from sun to sun strengthening the walls of the stockade and laying in supplies to withstand a siege. Only the most skillful hunters and woodsmen were permitted to go out for game. Others went out in large groups to gather wood, and they kept their rifles handy.

A tall, lean man named Simon Kenton, about twenty years old, went into the woods alone each day to watch for Indians. Simon was an excellent woodsman and well able to take care of himself. If an Indian army had approached, Simon would have given the settlers at least a few hours' warning, but he could not scout every ravine for little bands of warriors.

On the morning of April 14, Simon helped a boy open one of the heavy gates of the stockade to let the cows out. But Squire Boone's old cow Spot did not want to go out. She waddled a few steps and stopped, her nose in the air.

"Get along, Spot," the boy called.

Spot fidgeted and shook her head impatiently.

"That cow smells Injuns," Simon said.

Two men walked past. "What does a cow know about Injuns?" they said. They went out into the clearing.

"I don't like the looks of it," Simon said to the boy. "Let's chase the cows back into the stockade, and I'll go out and have a look around."

As they pushed the cows back through the gate, they heard a shout. One of the men who had just left was racing toward them. An Indian was scalping the other, not sixty yards from the gate.

Simon raised his long rifle and fired. The Indian dropped dead.

Simon calmly reloaded. As he did so, two other Indians leaped from the bushes to pick up the body of their fallen comrade.

Daniel Boone and others heard the shot and rushed out with rifles ready. Despite his long experience in Indian warfare, Daniel made a mistake. He ran toward the Indians. A dozen men, including Simon, followed him.

When they were about a hundred yards from the stockade, they heard warwhoops behind them. A party of warriors had dashed in from the side and cut them off from the stockade.

"Back to the gate!" Daniel ordered. "Charge them!"

Rifles crashed, and the air was filled with white smoke. There was no time to reload. Whites fought with rifle butts and Indians with tomahawks.

Simon Kenton was not one to waste powder, and not seeing a very good target he held his fire until the smoke cleared away. Then he saw that Daniel was down, and an Indian was running toward him with a scalping knife. Simon fired and the Indian fell.

Another Indian leaped at Daniel. Simon knocked him down with the rifle butt, thus saving Daniel's life twice in a couple of minutes.

The big Pennsylvania German, Mike Stoner, was in the thick of the fight, laying about him with his rifle, when a bullet hit his arm. He fell.

Another big man ran to help him up.

"Get away from me altogether," Mike roared. "We make too big a lump to shoot at." He got to his feet and staggered toward the fort.

The Indians ran for cover, carrying their dead and wounded. Simon picked up Daniel and carried him toward the stockade.

As soon as they could reload, the Indians opened fire from the bushes and canebrake. Bullets whistled past Simon's ears and kicked up dirt in front of him. Jemima Callaway, Daniel's daughter, ran from the stockade and helped Simon carry Daniel to safety.

Boonesborough was lucky that day. Only the man who

was scalped before the shooting began was dead. No one else was killed, but Daniel had a broken ankle and Mike Stoner a broken arm.

On July 4, before Daniel's ankle healed, a large force of Shawnee warriors surrounded Boonesborough. For two days bullets slapped against the logs of the stockade and flaming arrows struck cabin roofs. Inside the stockade, men fired through loopholes while women and children beat out the flames. Then the Indians stole away as silently as they had come.

Daniel knew that this was only a sample of what was to come. The Shawnees were testing the strength of the Kentucky whites.

Soon after this about two hundred riflemen arrived from Virginia and North Carolina, but only about fifty of them remained at Boonesborough. The others went to reinforce the garrisons at Harrodsburg and Logan's Station.

By January, 1778, all three Kentucky settlements were out of salt, which they used not only for seasoning but also for curing meat and hides. About thirty men from the three settlements went to Blue Licks and began the tedious work of making salt.

They filled big iron kettles with salty water from a spring and boiled off the water. About 800 gallons of water yielded a bushel of salt, but a bushel of salt was worth as much as a cow, so their work was profitable.

For nearly a month, all went well. Daniel Boone and his son-in-law, Flanders Callaway, went out in different directions each day to hunt for meat and watch for Indian signs.

Blue Licks was far north of Boonesborough and only

about a day's march from the Ohio River. It was right on the trail from the Shawnee country to the Kentucky settlements. But the men felt fairly safe because they did not expect a large Indian army to enter Kentucky in the middle of the winter.

One day early in February, Daniel Boone, hunting alone, killed a buffalo in a canebrake some five miles from the salt camp. He butchered the buffalo and put a heavy load of meat on the back of his saddle horse.

Snow was flying and the wind was very cold. Daniel's hands were numb, and he was in a hurry to get back to camp. Carelessly he thrust his long knife into its sheath without wiping the blood from the blade.

He was leading his horse along a narrow trail, past the upturned roots of a fallen tree, when the horse startled. Daniel looked back and saw the barrel of a long rifle moving in the bushes.

He grabbed his knife, planning to cut the thongs which held the meat on the horse's back, dump the load off, and gallop away on the horse. But the blood on his knife blade had frozen, and he could not pull it from the sheath. He dropped the reins and ran.

A rifle crashed and a bullet whined past him. Four Shawnee braves were sprinting after him with whoops. There was no good cover, and his tracks were plain in the snow so he could not hide. When the braves reached his horse, one of them cut the thongs, dumped the load, and mounted. Daniel could not outrun the horse.

Two more shots rang out. Daniel discovered a bullet had cut the strap which held his powder horn and the powder horn had fallen into the snow beside the trail. He could fire only one shot.

He knew escape was impossible. He stopped, leaned his rifle against a tree as a sign of surrender and waved at the Indians.

As the warriors came panting up to him, he remembered his old rule that Indians, like whites, treat you pretty much as you expect to be treated. "How d' do," he said, smiling.

The braves took his rifle and tried to yank his knife from the sheath. He helped them pry it loose. Then they said "How d' do," and shook hands.

This was like old times, when Captain Will had captured Boone and Stuart and scolded them for hunting. He hoped these Indians would merely march him north for a few days and turn him loose.

But such hopes vanished an hour later when the braves led him to a camp fire some thirty feet long. Around it sat more than a hundred Shawnees in war paint, and a few white men.

One of the braves who had captured Boone made a lengthy speech in a high sing-song voice, and Boone understood only the words "Boone, big chief of the Long Knives." The rest of the speech probably emphasized the bravery of the speaker and his companions and told how cunning they were to capture Boone.

Daniel hoped that the speaker also mentioned that the leader of the Long Knives showed no fear upon being captured. At the moment Daniel's life depended upon the impression he made. He must be calm, somewhat amused, careless of his own fate, but not quite insolent enough to provoke some young hothead into striking him with a tomahawk.

During the speech the braves sat motionless. Some spat

into the fire, indicating their contempt of the white chief. When the speech was finished, several older men arose, said "How d' do," and shook hands.

Boone knew this was no gesture of friendship, but merely a salute, recognizing Boone's rank. Indians sometimes shook hands with a respected captive before putting him to death.

Daniel recognized one of the braves. "Captain Will!" he exclaimed.

Captain Will stared at him with no sign of recognition.

With gestures and the few Shawnee words he knew, Boone reminded Captain Will of their previous meeting.

"You steal my horses," he said. "I steal them back. You steal them again. You put bell on my neck. I run away. You can't find me." He haw-hawed. This was a good opportunity to prove that he was not afraid to taunt his captors.

Captain Will remembered now, laughed, and shook hands again. This was a good omen.

One dark-skinned brave spoke to Boone in good English. His name was Pompey. He was a Negro and had been a slave of the whites, but had escaped and joined the Shawnees.

"Chief Blackfish wants to talk to you," Pompey said.

He led Boone to a short, powerfully built old man, with fierce, deep-set eyes. Boone knew that next to the aged Chief Cornstalk, Blackfish was the most important Shawnee chief.

"How d' do," Blackfish said. They shook hands. Blackfish studied Boone for a time, then gathered his robes about him and squatted. Boone also sat down. An old record tells of their conversation. Evidently Pompey acted as translator for this and other talks, although this is uncertain. "Who are the men at the salt springs?" Blackfish asked.

Boone hesitated. This was a blow. He had hoped the Indians did not know of the others.

"They are my men," he said finally.

"Good! Tomorrow morning we will surround their camp and kill them."

10

DANIEL THINKS FAST

"You come to kill my people because the redcoats paid you," Daniel Boone said to Chief Blackfish.

The chief did not change expressions. He spoke slowly. "That is not true. When the redcoats came to us and offered us much red paint and many guns to fight the Long Knives, we refused. Our great Chief Cornstalk went to the fort of the Long Knives on Mount Pleasant on the Ohio River and talked peace with the Long Knives. But the Long Knives murdered him and his son, although they came in peace, without arms. The spirit of Chief Cornstalk calls out from the grave for us to revenge his murder. He cannot rest until we take revenge."

Daniel knew that the Indians could surround the salt camp and take the men by surprise. It was unlikely that any one of them would escape to warn Boonesborough. The people of Boonesborough would not be expecting an attack in the dead of the winter. The stockade needed repairs. A war party this size could capture it by storm. If the women and children were not tomahawked, many of them would die from cold and exhaustion during the march north.

When he answered Blackfish, he spoke with great care.

"You come to kill my people because the redcoats paid you!"

The Long Knives who murdered Chief Cornstalk, he said, were not from Kentucky but belonged to another tribe. They were bad and dishonorable. If the Shawnee chiefs come to Kentucky to talk peace, the Kentucky Long Knives will spread a feast and talk honorably.

"But the Long Knives in Kentucky," he continued, "are tired of fighting the Shawnees. They cannot hunt or grow corn while the fighting goes on." He suggested that the Boonesborough Long Knives, with their women and children, might be willing to go north and live with the Shawnees in peace. But they could not go in winter. They would rather fight a battle than travel with their women and children in cold weather. Next summer would be different, he hinted. He spoke of the great number of riflemen at Boonesborough who were willing to fight if necessary.

Finally he suggested that he himself would go to the

salt camp and tell his men there to surrender peacefully, if the Indians would promise to treat them well and not make them run the gantlet. This was a form of punishment in which a prisoner was made to run between two facing lines of braves who struck him with tomahawks, clubs, or whatever they could find.

Boone said the men at the salt camp would go north now with Blackfish. Next summer he himself would lead Blackfish's men back to Boonesborough and tell all the people there to surrender.

Blackfish talked it over with the other chiefs. Then he told Boone that the men at the salt camp would not have to run the gantlet if they surrendered without firing a shot.

The next morning Boone walked into the salt camp. Some fifty steps behind him came three Indians, with rifles pointed at his back. The men of the camp seized their rifles, but Daniel called to them that they were surrounded and resistance was useless.

Then he explained to them that they would have to surrender to save their own lives and the lives of their families in the stockades. "You will not be tortured or forced to run the gantlet," he said.

The men stacked their arms. The Indians came in from all sides and bound their hands behind them. Daniel was relieved to see that Flanders Callaway was not there. He would carry the word to Boonesborough.

Then the Indians sat down for a council of war. A young brave arose and made a speech. Pompey, sitting next to Boone, translated but in such a low tone that only Boone could hear.

The Long Knives in the fort, the young brave said,

invited Chief Cornstalk in for a talk and then murdered him. Chief Cornstalk's spirit cried for revenge. Now the Shawnees had thirty Long Knives who should be roasted to death, one at a time.

Daniel looked quickly at Blackfish. The old chief had his usual stern expression, but Daniel could see no sign of surprise or anger on the copper features. A snowflake settled on Blackfish's big Roman nose and melted slowly. The chief looked more like a statue than a living being.

Daniel knew that an Indian chief was not an absolute ruler of his people, but was regarded as a father or older brother. In the heat of battle he commanded, but at other times he only advised. If the majority of the warriors wanted to kill their prisoners, Blackfish would be helpless to protect them.

Daniel had about the same degree of authority over his own men. They followed his advice usually, but they felt no compulsion to do so. In battle, white frontiersmen were not nearly so well disciplined as were the Indians.

Another brave arose. The Long Knives, he said, were no good. Not only did they kill Chief Cornstalk who visited them in peace. They crept up on villages and killed women and children. They could fight only when they were hiding behind a fence of big logs. In the forest a hundred Shawnees could defeat a thousand palefaces. He told of many battles that the Indians had won when they were outnumbered. The Long Knives were cowards and should be killed without all this argument.

An older chief arose now and spoke calmly. He agreed that white men had done bad things. They could not stand against Shawnees in battle. They could not bear pain. They were weak like children. When they were captured and burned, they cried out shamelessly. He was surprised to see that Boone, the chief of these pale worms, was not crying. But on the other hand, the Shawnees must be wise. They now had much booty and many captives. They would have great glory when they got home. The redcoats would pay much money for these captives. The Shawnees should take these men to the redcoats at Detroit. Next summer the Shawnees could easily capture the other Long Knives in Kentucky.

A white man stood up next. He was a Frenchman but was now acting as a British agent. Speaking in Shawnee, he said it made no difference whether the Shawnees killed these captives or not, but they should go immediately to attack the log houses down south. He laughed at reports that Boonesborough had many riflemen. There were only a few men behind the log walls, he said.

He was right, but Boone hoped the Indians would not believe him.

Finally, after many had spoken, Blackfish signaled to Boone that he was to speak. Boone stood up.

"Brothers," he said, and Pompey translated into Shawnee, "what I have promised you I can much better fulfill in the spring than now. Then the weather will be warm and the women and children can travel."

He told the Shawnees that if they killed these young men, the Great Spirit would be displeased, and the Shawnees would not have success in hunting or war.

The other Kentuckians, their hands bound, were huddled in a little group in the center of the great circle of warriors. Unable to understand Shawnee, they had no idea that the Shawnees were debating whether or not to burn them at the stake. Now, as Boone spoke, they stiffened their spines and stared at him in horror and amazement.

Boone continued, telling the Shawnees that these young men would make good warriors and hunters if they were permitted to join the Shawnees.

"They have done you no harm and they surrendered as I advised them. I told them to surrender only because you said they would be treated well. Spare them, and the Great Spirit will smile upon you." He sat down.

Then the matter was put to a vote. A war club was passed around. If a warrior struck the ground with it, he was voting to kill the whites. Boone kept count. Fifty-nine struck the ground. Sixty-one did not. Blackfish's policy had been approved by a narrow margin.

The young warriors glared at Boone with hatred. He knew that if he or the other captives did anything to arouse the contempt of the warriors, another vote would be taken, with different results.

The Indians now unbound their captives and put them to work loading plunder on the horses. Blackfish stood with arms folded. Ordinarily when work was to be done, Boone worked harder than anyone else, but he decided he must now play the part of chief. He folded his arms.

After the horses were loaded, a fierce-looking young Shawnee handed Boone a brass kettle and said something in contemptuous tones.

"What's he saying?" Boone asked Pompey.

"He says you are to carry this kettle on the march."

"I am to carry a kettle," Boone said. He laughed and threw the kettle down into the snow.

The young brave leaped at him with a roar.

Boone swung and connected solidly with the brave's

chin. There was a pop. The brave's feet flew up, and he landed on the back of his neck in a snowbank.

There was complete silence. Everyone stood staring. The fallen brave sat up with a dazed look on his face and rubbed his chin.

Then an old chief whooped with laughter. The other Shawnees joined. The forest rang with their mirth. The brave got to his feet, stared at Boone for a moment, then he too laughed.

After this, the young braves eyed Boone with wonder. They had always taken it for granted that white men were weaklings and cowards. But if the white chief could knock a Shawnee flat on his back, it proved that there was some good in the white race. As the march began, there was much laughter in the ranks.

They marched north at good speed. Boone's men were all strong and in good health, so they could keep up the pace. Toward evening the column halted, and the Indians gave the captives a good supper. But when the meal was over, Boone noticed that the Indians were clearing a wide path in the snow and arming themselves with heavy sticks, deer antlers, and other blunt weapons. He knew what this meant.

"Tell Chief Blackfish," he said to Pompey, "that he promised my men would not have to run the gantlet."

"Chief Blackfish," Pompey said, "remembers his promise and will keep it. The gantlet is for you. He did not promise that you would not have to run."

Boone admitted that he had forgotten to mention himself.

"Tell your chief," he said, "that he is an honorable man, and I am glad that I can run the gantlet. Before I join the

Boone lowered his head and charged through the gantlet

Shawnees I want to know whether they are weak like children or are strong men and can hit hard."

Pompey translated this speech in a loud voice, and the Shawnees laughed happily. They would be glad to show the white chief how hard they could hit.

Boone took his place, lowered his head and charged. As he entered the gantlet he zig-zagged, so that he was too far from one man and too close to another to get the full force of their blows. Then he stopped, leaped forward, dodged. The Indians hit and missed, sometimes striking each other in their confusion. One brave stepped out in front of Boone to get in a good blow, but Boone butted him in the chest and knocked him over backwards. Again the woods rang with Shawnee laughter.

It took a long time to get through the line this way, but Boone probably got fewer solid blows than he would have got if he had sprinted.

When it was over, the Shawnees helped him bind his bloody head and shook hands with him, this time in real friendship.

That night, and every night thereafter on the trip, the whites slept most uncomfortably. As one of them later wrote, each man's arms were tied behind him, "a rope or buffalo's tug tied fast around his middle and then made fast to an Indian on each side of him, and the one around his arms was made to go around his neck, and tied fast to a tree, and in that position he had to sleep on the snow."

For ten days they trudged in bitter cold. Some of the Indians suffered from frozen ears, but they did not complain. Not accustomed to or properly dressed for long marches in winter weather, the Indians had a worse time than the whites.

About half of the captives imitated Boone, marching along stolidly, pretending they were neither tired nor cold. The others complained and snarled at each other and the Indians. One, Andrew Johnson, played a game of his own. He was a tiny fellow, and looked like a young boy. When he was given a load, he fell down and cried. He seemed not to understand what the Indians wanted him to do. He was such a pathetic creature that the Indians took pity on him and let him stagger along without carrying anything. Boone was greatly amused by this, because he knew that Andrew was strong as an ox and very shrewd.

After they crossed the Ohio River, game was scarce, and often there was nothing to eat except the bark of white oak and slippery elm. The Indians divided the food equally and were just as hungry as their captives.

On the eleventh day they stopped and the Indians began painting their faces and fixing themselves up. Pompey explained that they were near the great Shawnee town of Chillicothe and were preparing for a grand march into town.

Dozens of Indian women came from the town and picked up most of the booty, so the braves could march in without burdens. The white captives were given big loads. Those captives who had complained during the march were stripped naked and given extra loads. Boone felt sorry for them, but there was nothing he could do. He and little Andrew Johnson did not have to carry anything.

The town consisted of several hundred wigwams and a big council house. Singing and whooping, the warriors marched into town and did a war dance. However, only the women and children watched. Braves of the town who had not been on the expedition remained in the council house.

It was plainly a great occasion. Never had a war party returned with so many captives since Braddock's defeat twenty-three years before.

When the war dance was over, the warriors took their captives into the council house. Here the naked ones were permitted to put their clothes on. There was a long pow-wow with speeches and arguments. Pompey explained the proceedings to Boone and translated some of the speeches. Late in the afternoon the session was adjourned for a feast. The captives were not invited to the feast but were well fed.

The next day the powwow was resumed, and votes were taken. Boone was voted a fine fellow, and Blackfish himself announced that he intended to adopt Boone as a son. Other warriors asked to adopt those whites who had behaved well on the trip. The complaining whites were voted "no-good." They were to be sold to the British at Detroit.

The "no-goods" were happy. They had been smart to complain, even though they had to march into town naked. It was much safer to be a prisoner of the British than of the Indians.

Little Andrew Johnson was a special problem. It seemed unlikely that the British would pay anything for a foolish child. But one old chief said that he and his wife wanted to adopt Andrew. They had lost a son and were lonesome. They said they would treat Andrew well, and maybe he would grow up into a warrior.

Blackfish then announced that he and forty warriors

would take the "no-goods" to Detroit for sale. He would also take Daniel Boone along, as a sort of prize exhibit to impress the British. He would of course bring Boone back for formal adoption into his family.

While Blackfish, Boone, and the others were absent on this Detroit trip, little Andrew destroyed most of the good will which Boone had built up and made life very difficult and dangerous for the other captives. But they did not blame Andrew for what he did.

11

DANIEL BECOMES BIG TURTLE

The old chief who had adopted Andrew began training him almost immediately. He put a light load in a rifle, showed Andrew how to aim, and asked him to shoot at a tree. Little Andrew raised the heavy gun, closed his eyes, and pulled the trigger. The gun kicked him over backward. The Indians laughed.

"Pequolly," they said, which meant "Little-shut-his-eyes." From then on, Andrew's name was Pequolly.

The old chief tried again, but poor Pequolly could not learn to shoot. The Indian children liked to tease him.

"Pequolly," they would ask, "which way Kentucky?"

Pequolly would look up at the sky, think a while, and point in the wrong direction. The old chief and his wife were sad. Their adopted son, it seemed, was not only afraid but weak-minded.

One morning Pequolly was gone. The old chief could not find his best rifle, powder horn and bullet pouch. He was in despair.

"I scolded Pequolly," he said, "and that's why he ran away. He will die in the woods and wolves will eat him."

Searching parties were sent in all directions, for there was no telling which way Pequolly would wander. They could find no trace of him. After several days, when they were sure he was dead, they gave up the search.

A few weeks later a little party of Shawnee hunters, who had camped near Chillicothe, were awakened at dawn by rifle fire.

"Hey," they called, "we are Shawnees!" They supposed that another Shawnee party had mistaken them for enemies.

The rifle fire continued. Bullets kicked up ashes of the camp fire and cut twigs from bushes. They crawled to safety, very much puzzled. When the shooting stopped they looked around and found that their seven pack horses were gone.

Returning to Chillicothe, they told their story in the council house, and the chiefs wondered what tribe would have the courage to send a party into the heart of Shawnee territory to steal horses.

A few days later the mystery was solved. A lone hunter arrived and said he had seen Pequolly and five other whites take seven horses across the Ohio into Kentucky.

Now the old resentment against the whites flared up again. Young braves made speeches. White men, they said, are foxes, weak and timid but full of beastly cunning. Pequolly is no child, but a dangerous man. He found his way back to Kentucky and now is leading raiding parties into the Shawnee land.

The old men admitted they had been fooled by Pequolly, but they said the wrong magic had been used when Pequolly was adopted.

"The white blood was not all washed out of him, and so he betrayed us."

Young braves said it was dangerous and foolish to

befriend a white man. He can't be trusted until he is dead. White men work in the fields like women. They skulk through the woods to steal our horses. They do not have the virtues of Indians.

Meanwhile Blackfish had reached the British fort at Detroit and sold his no-good prisoners. The British commander was much impressed by Boone and offered a huge ransom for him, but Blackfish refused. Boone, he said, would become a great Shawnee warrior.

The British commander gave Boone a handsome suit of clothes. But Blackfish reasoned that since Boone was to be his son, it would look bad if Boone returned to Chillicothe with better clothes than Blackfish himself had. The young warriors would ridicule him. So Blackfish took the suit. Boone did not object. He had no use for an elegant costume.

When Blackfish and Boone returned to Chillicothe, they found a bad situation. Young braves said openly that white captives should be killed and the Shawnees should march immediately into Kentucky and destroy the settlements.

But the old men did not want war if it could be avoided. They had seen too much of war.

In order to keep his position as Big Chief, Blackfish had to please both factions. He proposed that the Shawnees continue to treat their captives well and adopt them into the tribe. Then when warm weather came, the Shawnees would raise a large army and march into Kentucky. If the whites surrendered, as Boone had promised, all would be well and no lives lost. If they did not surrender, the Shawnees would destroy them.

The young braves did not like this compromise very well, but they agreed to it with angry mutterings.

Blackfish made a big ceremony of Boone's adoption into the tribe. One afternoon an old Indian came to Blackfish's wigwam, where Boone lived, bringing a piece of bark with a little pile of ashes on it.

Boone sat down. The old man dipped his fingers in the ashes, took hold of a lock of Boone's hair, and yanked it out. The ashes on his fingers helped him get a firm grip on the hair. The pain was intense but Boone did not wince. The hair-pulling continued until only a scalp lock was left on top of Boone's head. Then the old man braided a string of beads and silver ornaments into the scalp lock.

Boone then took off his clothes and put on a breech clout, and the old man painted Boone's face and body with the colors and patterns of the tribe. Boone put on silver bracelets and armbands and other ornaments.

Blackfish led him outside and called the alarm signal. People came running from all wigwams. While Boone shivered in the raw spring wind, Blackfish made a speech, explaining that Boone was to become his son.

After that the most prominent old women of the town took Boone down to the river and scrubbed him from head to foot to "wash out the white blood." He was handed a staff and instructed to march to the council house.

Here a pile of presents awaited him, including hunting clothes, blankets, a ruffled shirt, leggings decorated with ribbons and beads, and a pair of moccasins. He put on some of this finery. His face was again painted and red feathers were tied in his scalp lock. He was given a pipe and tobacco and a tomahawk.

Now all the warriors of the town marched in, dressed

in their best garments. Everyone sat down on the benches lining the wall. Pipes were lighted, and the warriors sat for a time in silence. Boone lighted his pipe and took a few puffs, for ceremonial reasons, but he did not enjoy it because he was not a tobacco user.

Finally Blackfish arose and made a speech. Boone

Blackfish explained that Boone was to become his son

could now understand Shawnee fairly well and did not need a translator.

Blackfish said that every drop of white blood had been washed out of Boone.

"You are taken into the Shawnee nation and initiated into a warlike tribe," he said. "You are adopted into a great family."

Assuring Boone that he was now a Shawnee, Blackfish concluded, "You are one of us by an old strong law and custom. My son, you have nothing to fear. We are now under the same obligation to love, support, and defend you that we are to love and defend one another. Therefore you are to consider yourself one of our people."

Boone was then given the name of Sheltowee, which meant "big turtle," and was personally introduced to each warrior.

That night there was a great feast of venison and corn, maple sugar, bear fat, and hominy.

But soon the tribe was to suffer hunger, partly because of the large amount of meat consumed at this and other adoption feasts.

Boone was now officially a Shawnee but he was not easy in his mind. He knew that most of the young men still considered him white and hated him for that reason, and even the old chiefs looked upon him with suspicion. He was not afraid of being murdered, because primitive people do not kill members of their own tribe, but he knew that any warrior, young or old, would shoot him if he tried to run away, for that would prove that he did not really belong to the tribe. When he left the town for a squirrel hunt, one or more of the young men followed him, watching every move that he made.

Old Blackfish treated his new son with every kindness but he was shrewd enough to know what was in Boone's mind. Blackfish kept careful count of the bullets he gave to Boone, and when Boone returned from a hunt, Blackfish asked how many shots he had fired and what he had killed. Generally Boone had to tell the truth, because he knew Indian scouts had watched him. However, he devised ways to deceive his watchers.

Sometimes, while gazing into a tree pretending to look for squirrels, he cut a bullet in two. With a half-bullet he could kill a squirrel or turkey. Of course, he had to be careful not to bring home a turkey with a half-bullet lodged in its body.

Often he made an elaborate pretense of eating a piece of jerked venison, but he actually stuffed the meat into the sleeve of his hunting shirt. This way he slowly accumulated a little store of food and bullets which he kept hidden in a leather sack under his shirt. His life was in danger every minute he carried this sack.

One day on a hunt, while sharp eyes were watching from a distance, he sat down beside a tree and gazed upward for a long time. Meanwhile his hands, out of sight of the watchers, were very busy digging a hole and burying the sack.

On days that he did not hunt, he busied himself about the town. Remembering the skill he had learned in his father's blacksmith shop, he repaired rifles for the Indians. Even without a forge and anvil he could sometimes fix a gun which the Indians considered beyond repair. To them he seemed to have magic powers.

Once they brought him a rifle without a stock. He shook his head over this job, saying it would take a long time, or maybe it could never be fixed. He laid the rifle aside until the Indians had forgotten about it, then hid it in the woods.

Often Boone engaged in shooting matches and other games, but he was careful not to win too often. His adopted mother, Blackfish's wife, advised him. "My son, you must not win today," she would say. "Young men would be angry."

Remembering his own experience with Saucy Jack, years before in the Yadkin Valley, Boone took her advice.

12

A RACE FOR LIFE

Boone's Shawnee was now so good that he could always make himself understood. However, children often laughed happily at the way he talked. He joined in the fun and deliberately made mistakes to keep people in good humor.

He particularly liked the children, and some of them became his special friends. He traded various trinkets he had been given for maple syrup or sugar and gave these sweets to his young friends. Imitating his speech, they called it "molas'."

The Shawnees did not live an easy life. Sometimes there was nothing at all to eat and people grew weak with hunger. This may have been due partly to the fact that the whites had killed much of the game in Kentucky, so the Shawnees could not lay up a large supply of jerked meat for the winter. But mostly it was due to the Indian way of life.

All tribes which depend largely upon hunting and very little upon farming go through periods of hunger when game is scarce. If the Shawnees had been willing and able to farm rather than hunt, they would have been more prosperous. But people cannot and will not change their ways until they are forced to do so by great developments over which they have little control.

Possibly Daniel Boone suggested to Blackfish, during one of their long conversations around a fire in the wigwam, that the Shawnee men should help the women in the field, so the tribe would have more corn for the winter months. But if he did, we can be sure Blackfish rejected the idea. The Shawnees, like other hunting people, believed that farming was women's work and that it would weaken a man for hunting and fighting.

Blackfish's wife would have been scandalized at the idea. The suggestion that a man should plant corn as she did would have been, in her opinion, an insult to Shawnee men.

Boone knew that Shawnee men were not lazy. When the tribe was hungry they went hunting even while blizzards were raging. Sometimes they staggered into camp and collapsed with exhaustion after a long unsuccessful hunt. It was a matter of pride with them never to spare themselves. But they had been brought up to feel that any man who did women's work was a contemptible wretch.

Boone himself did not consider field work humiliating, but he disliked it, so he was able to understand the Indians' point of view. He was somewhat like an Indian, not because any white blood had been "washed out" of him, but because he had been brought up to honor hunting above all other occupations.

After one period of semistarvation, when the whole village went hungry for days, a party of braves marched in carrying several deer. The women then brewed a vile concoction for everyone to drink before eating. Boone swallowed a little of the stuff and became sick at his stomach. But the Indians said that if he did not drink it, the fresh deer meat would make him sick. Soon his appetite returned and he ate a big meal of venison without any ill effects.

Considering everything, Boone enjoyed life as a Shawnee. He would have enjoyed it more if he had not been forced always to deceive the Indians and prepare to escape. Some of the other white men who had been adopted into the tribe were apparently content and planned to remain Shawnees the rest of their lives.

But Boone knew he had to escape. His wife and children could not live this sort of life. To save his scalp he had promised Blackfish that all the Boonesborough people would join the Shawnee tribe or at least agree to go to Detroit and surrender to the British. But he knew that this could not happen.

The life of the Kentucky pioneers was probably harder and more dangerous than was the life of the Shawnees. Blackfish felt that any sensible man would rather live the free life of the Indian, full of color and adventure, than the drab life of the white pioneer who had to build fences, milk cows, and plant corn. But Boone knew that the white settlers would fight to the death rather than change their habits, customs, and way of making a living, as they would have to do if they joined the Shawnee tribe.

Boone also knew that the whites would finally win the battle for Kentucky, not because they were braver or more intelligent than the Indians, which they were not, but because they had a better way of making a living.

One day a party of Shawnee hunters arrived at Chillicothe and reported that they had been ambushed by white men, led by Pequolly. The whites had killed and scalped several Shawnees.

Anger swept through the tribe. There was a long war council. Again young warriors made speeches and said that every white man should be roasted. They did not say outright that Boone and the other adopted members of the tribe were white, but as they spoke they glared at their palefaced brothers with hatred. They wanted to organize a party to go immediately to attack Boonesborough.

Blackfish, the skillful politician, saw that something must be done. He said that the Shawnees were not yet ready to go to Kentucky. But he proposed that a war party be sent against the fort where Chief Cornstalk had been killed. The young men agreed. A war party was hastily assembled and sent off.

A fortnight later this party returned and admitted defeat. Many fine warriors had been killed by the "cowardly whites who hide behind log walls." Again there was bitter oratory against the Long Knives who "planted corn like women and were afraid to fight in the forest."

Blackfish knew that the march into Kentucky could not be delayed much longer, so he gave orders for a big war party to assemble. He still had hopes that his policy would succeed, that Boone would persuade the Kentucky settlers to surrender. But he probably had his doubts, and he may have guessed that Boone planned to escape.

One day when Boone was in the forest with a small party of warriors he saw what he thought might be a chance to escape. The warriors had carelessly put down their rifles and walked away a little distance to engage in wrestling matches. Boone hastily removed the bullets from their guns.

Just as he finished this task, the warriors returned and saw him laying down a gun. Instantly suspicious, they asked him what he was doing.

He hesitated. He knew that as soon as one of them fired a rifle, they would all know by the sound of the explosion that the bullet had been removed. They would know that he had planned to make a run for it.

An inspiration came to him. "I'm going to run away," he said.

They picked up their rifles. "No you're not," they said.

He walked about forty steps then broke into a run. They raised their rifles and fired. He stopped, pretending to catch the bullets in the tail of his hunting shirt and walked back to them.

"Here are your bullets," he said.

It was a great joke on the warriors. It served them right for being so careless as to leave their rifles unguarded. It also seemed to prove that Boone did not want to escape. The story went around, and the whole tribe laughed. Boone was better liked.

Meanwhile preparations were being made for the march on Kentucky. Warriors from other villages arrived, until more than five hundred men were assembled. In the council house the chiefs met daily and made plans. Women assembled a great store of provisions.

Soon a three-day fast would begin, during which the warriors would drink only a bitter concoction and would not sit down or even lean against anything from dawn until nightfall. After the fast, the long march would begin.

Boone knew that he must try to escape now, no matter what chances he took.

One morning a party of warriors, followed by women leading pack horses, went to hunt a bear. Boone went along but did not have a rifle.

After they had gone a few miles, they scared up a large flock of turkeys. The birds sailed a few hundred yards and settled in trees. The warriors hurried after them.

This was the chance Boone had been waiting for. When shots rang out in the woods ahead, indicating that the warriors were busy with the turkeys, Boone cut the thongs and unloaded one of the horses.

Blackfish's wife was among the women. "My son," she cried, "what are you doing?"

"I am going to see my wife and children," he told her.

"You cannot go. Blackfish will be angry." She was almost in tears.

"I must."

"You will starve in the woods."

"I have some supplies hidden away," he told her. "I am very sorry to leave you and my father, Blackfish, and all my Shawnee brothers and sisters." This was the truth. He regretted leaving them, but he had no choice. He mounted and galloped away, while the women ran after the warriors, crying the alarm.

Boone plunged through the woods to the place where he had hidden his leather sack of dried meat and ammunition and his stockless rifle. Then he rode south all that day and night. Fortunately he met no Shawnee hunters. When the horse was too tired to travel fast, he turned it loose and ran on afoot.

Boone was then nearly forty-four years old, but few athletes in their prime could have kept up with him.

He had a slight advantage over the Shawnees pursuing him because he had taken the best horse. Also they would have to trail him, because they did not know which of the many routes he would take. To confuse this trail he sometimes waded in swift-flowing streams.

At the end of the second day he came to the Ohio River which was swollen with the spring rains. Here he might have been trapped, for he could not swim, but he had a rare bit of luck. After ranging along the bank for some miles, he came upon an old canoe with a hole in its bottom. Working very fast, he plugged the hole and paddled across.

On the third day he passed Blue Licks, where he had been captured five months before. The march from Blue Licks to Chillicothe at that time had taken eleven days.

He was now in fairly safe territory and was very hungry, having eaten his little supply of dried meat long before. He found a piece of wood which was about the right size and tied it to the breech of his stockless rifle. Then he killed a buffalo and had a feast. He cut out the tongue and carried it with him as a present for his eight-year-old son, Daniel Morgan Boone.

At the end of the fourth day he limped into Boonesborough, having traveled 160 miles through the wilderness at the rate of 40 miles a day.

It was a dismal homecoming. Of his own kin, only Jemima and her husband, Flanders Callaway, and Squire Boone were there to greet him. His wife Rebecca had given him up for dead and had taken the children back to North Carolina.

Boone limped into Boonesborough at the end of the fourth day

The settlers crowded around him. Men shook hands and women cried. They seemed weary and discouraged. Only Jemima was blooming and full of energy.

She waved the others away. "Daddy has to rest," she said. "Bring chairs and a table, and some blankets," she ordered.

She led him to his cabin. It was bare and empty, but in a few minutes people came bringing enough furniture and utensils for a half-dozen cabins.

Daniel waved most of them away. "Don't need all this stuff," he said. He handed Jemima the buffalo tongue. "I brought this for the boy," he said, "but it'll likely spoil before I see him."

He sat down wearily, smiling at the excited people around him. There was a soft plop and he looked down to see a cat in his lap. It was the Boone family cat and the special property of little Daniel Morgan Boone, but had been left behind when the family went east.

All of his life Daniel remembered the greeting of this cat.

13

THE SHAWNEES COME

When Daniel Boone arrived, bringing word that the Indians would soon attack, Boonesborough was in no condition to defend itself.

Many of the settlers had fled east, leaving only a dozen men, about a dozen boys big enough to aim a rifle, and a few women and children. The gates of the stockade were ready to collapse, and many logs in the walls had rotted. Two-story blockhouses had been built at only two of the four corners.

There were many stumps in the clearing around the stockade, and weeds had grown up around them. A warrior could creep up at night and hide behind one of these stumps, and from there he could fire at loopholes in the wall. There was one shallow well inside the stockade, but it did not provide enough water for even the people to drink, let alone the cattle and horses which would be shut up there if the Indians attacked.

A hundred warriors charging the stockade from all sides at once could have captured it with few losses.

Daniel Boone had one of the settlers write a letter, which he signed, to military authorities in Virginia asking them to send reinforcements as soon as possible. Of course, it would be months before such a force could arrive from Virginia. He also sent messages to the other Kentucky settlements, Logan's Station and Harrodsburg, pointing out that if Boonesborough fell, they would be next. He asked them to send every man they could spare.

Then he and the others set about repairing the gates, strengthening the walls and building two more blockhouses. They started digging a new well but quit digging before they struck water, because other things had to be done first.

About fifteen men and boys arrived from Logan's Station and a few came from Harrodsburg, bringing the strength of the garrison to about thirty men and twenty boys. But the total length of the stockade walls was about 900 feet, so that each man, with a boy or woman to load for him, would have to defend thirty feet of wall.

If three or four hundred Indians charged the walls from all sides at once, the whites could hope to kill only twenty or thirty of them, and the others would swarm over the walls with knives and tomahawks.

If the Indians maintained a long siege, the whites would have to surrender for lack of water and food. Or if the Indians got even one cannon from the British, they could batter down the stockade walls in a few hours.

The people of Boonesborough considered these possibilities and knew that their own chances of living through the summer were not very great. But they were too busy to worry much about death. If they had had less work to do, they might have become panic-stricken and fled.

Daniel wanted very much to see his wife and family, but he could not leave Boonesborough at the time of its greatest danger. He was glad that Rebecca and the children were not there. At least he would not have to worry about them.

After a month of the most strenuous work, the walls of the stockade were in good shape and two new blockhouses were finished except for the roofs.

On July 17 someone heard a faint cry from across the river and saw a man in rags wave his arms and fall at the water's edge. The alarm was sounded. Boone and other riflemen stood on the bank while someone paddled over in a canoe to investigate. The ragged man proved to be William Hancock, one of the men who had been captured with Boone at Blue Licks and adopted into the Shawnee tribe.

Hancock was hardly conscious when they carried him into the stockade, but a few hours later he was able to tell his story. He had slipped out of Chillicothe in the night and had spent nine days covering the distance Boone had traveled in four.

He said that after Boone's escape, the Shawnees had postponed the attack, waiting for the arrival of additional supplies from the British at Detroit. Hancock had talked with a British officer who told him that the British were sending four cannon. Hancock had attended the council where final plans were made, and the chiefs there said that more than four hundred warriors would begin the march in just three weeks.

Nine days of that time had already elapsed, but it would take the Indians twelve or fifteen days to reach Boonesborough, so the attack would come in a little over three weeks.

If the British kept their promise to provide cannon,

and if the Indians were able to transport the cannon to Kentucky, Boonesborough was doomed. Unless, of course, a large force of riflemen arrived from Virginia.

The stockade was now in good repair and there was not much to do. Boone grew restless. He could not sit still and wait for something to happen. He and twenty others saddled horses and rode north.

After they crossed the Ohio they proceeded very cautiously, keeping away from trails where they might meet war parties. They could not kill game for fear their shots would be heard, but each had brought along a sack of parched corn.

As they approached Chillicothe, by a round-about way, they discovered that the Indian army was already on the march, so they followed it, spying whenever possible. Once, sneaking through the woods behind this army and far off to the side, they ran into a party of about thirty warriors. There was a sharp fight in which one Indian was killed. The others fled.

A few days later they became so hungry that they decided one shot would not make much difference, so they killed a buffalo and feasted. They crossed the Ohio not far behind the army, and the next day, while the army was camped at Blue Licks, they slipped past it. On September fifth they rode into Boonesborough and announced that the Indians would arrive the following morning.

That night everybody worked furiously, storing up water and making other last-minute preparations.

The next morning Daniel instructed everyone to be calm and lazy if they went outside the stockade.

"Don't let them think we are worried," he said. "If

you're out where they can see you, pretend you don't care where they are or what they do."

They let the cows out as usual. Squire Boone's old cow Spot was nervous, but they urged her through the gate, and she evidently decided that if people were not scared, why should she be.

Most of the people stayed inside, fearing they would show their excitement if they went out. Every bucket, tub, barrel, or pot in the stockade was full of water, so that no one had to go to the spring.

About ten o'clock Moses and Isaiah Boone, young sons of Squire, mounted their ponies and rode out to the river to let the ponies drink. Daniel, rifle in hand, strolled along beside them. It was a warm morning and a blue haze hung over the trees of the surrounding forest.

Because of Daniel's calm manner, the boys were not at all worried. Perhaps they forgot that Indians were expected. As the ponies drank, Daniel saw a party of men some distance away, walking toward the fort and carrying two flags. The boys saw them also.

"The soldiers are coming from Virginia," they cried. "Let's ride to meet them."

"No," Daniel said, "they're not from Virginia. Let's go back. And don't hurry."

In about half an hour a lone figure approached, carrying a big white flag. From one of the corner blockhouses Daniel studied him.

"It's Pompey," he said, "the Negro Shawnee. Let me do the talking."

Pompey approached within hailing distance and sat down comfortably on a rail fence which surrounded the corn patch.

"Hello!" he shouted. "Is Captain Boone there?"

No answer.

Pompey called again.

"Yes," Boone called.

"We've come to take you to Detroit," Pompey said. "I've got letters for you from the British commander."

"Bring them to the gate," Daniel replied.

Pompey hesitated.

"Sheltowee, come out." Boone recognized the voice of Chief Blackfish, calling from the woods.

Boone conferred with others in the stockade.

"I'd better go and talk with them," he said.

"We'll never see you again," someone remarked.

"I think I'll be safe enough," Boone said. "There's just a chance that we can argue with them for a long time, until reinforcements arrive. If they have cannon, we can't hold out an hour. It's better to take a chance on argument."

With some misgivings the others agreed.

Boone called to Blackfish and agreed to meet him at a certain stump. Then he walked out alone.

People in the stockade watched him walk out of rifle range. They saw the Indians spread down a blanket. They saw Boone sit down.

"That's the last of Daniel Boone," one of the men said.

14

SHOTS END A PEACE CONFERENCE

Perhaps Boone himself wondered if he would ever see the inside of the stockade again, but he adopted a careless, even friendly attitude as he shook hands with Blackfish.

"How d' do," Blackfish said. "Why did you run away from me?"

"I wanted to see my wife and children. I could not stay longer."

Blackfish shook his head sadly. "You should have said so. I would let you go any time."

Blackfish had never lied to Boone, and now he might well be telling the truth. Perhaps it would have fitted in with Blackfish's plans to let Boone return to Boonesborough. There was no telling what went on in the clever mind of the old chief.

Boone was embarrassed. The Shawnees had treated him well and now perhaps had only the friendliest intentions.

To cover his embarrassment, he decided to chide Blackfish in a friendly manner. "I was in your country not long ago, and I met some of your young men who want to kill white men. But they ran away fast. Why did they not stay and kill us?"

Blackfish showed no resentment. He clapped his hands

rapidly to indicate that shots came too fast, from every direction, and the young men did not know what was happening.

Blackfish then handed Boone a letter from the British commander at Detroit. The commander reminded Boone that he had promised to surrender and said that the young Indians were hard to control. The commander hoped Boone would be sensible and avoid a massacre.

Boone realized that from the Indian's point of view, his own behavior had been dishonest. He did not enjoy telling Blackfish that the Boonesborough people would not surrender. He remembered that one of the Boonesborough men, William Bailey Smith, had been a major in the Virginia militia before the Revolution and still had his scarlet uniform.

"I was gone so long from here," Boone said, "that the Big Chief in Virginia sent out a new commander, and I am no longer captain here. The new captain is not willing to surrender, although I want him to."

"Go and get him," Blackfish said.

Boone went back to the stockade and soon fetched out Major Smith in his scarlet coat and three-cornered hat with big ostrich plumes. Smith looked very much like a great commander.

When negotiations were resumed, Boone kept still and Smith shook his head. The argument went on a long time. Blackfish and the other chiefs were patient.

At one point Blackfish complained that the Long Knives had killed off all the game hereabouts and the Indian warriors were hungry.

"Kill our cattle when you need meat," Boone said, "but don't waste anything."

After several hours, Boone and Smith returned to the stockade for a conference with the other settlers.

"I'm not going to take all the responsibility," Boone said. "If we surrender, the Indians will probably take us to Detroit safely. If we don't, there will be a fight. If we lose, we will all be scalped. Make up your minds."

Squire Boone said he would never surrender, but would fight until he died. Most of the others said the same.

"Well, I'll die with the rest of you," Boone declared.

That afternoon Colonel Callaway, father of Betsey and Fanny, went out with Boone and Major Smith for another conference. The Indians spread panther skins on the ground, within rifle range of the stockade.

Blackfish and other chiefs spoke for the Indians. A Frenchman named De Quindre represented the British commander at Detroit. Warriors stood around holding branches over the heads of the delegates.

Blackfish said he would like to be introduced to Mrs. Boone and the wives of the other white captains. Boone hastily explained that white women were very much afraid of Indians and could not be persuaded to come outside the stockade.

Then Blackfish presented several buffalo tongues as a present for the white women.

Major Smith, as "commander" of the stockade, pretended to oppose surrender because it would be so hard to transport women and children to Detroit.

"I brought forty horses," Blackfish said, "so they can ride in comfort."

After a long talk, the settlers said they would give their answer the next day.

When Boone, Smith, and Callaway went back to the

stockade, Boone explained the situation to the others.

"Blackfish brought forty horses to carry the women and children," he said. "If he thinks we have forty women and children here, he must think we have hundreds of men. Maybe that explains why the Indians are willing to negotiate."

The settlers decided to prove to Blackfish that he was

The settlers promised an answer the next day

right. Women and children put on men's hats or coonskin caps. Even shovels and brooms were dressed to look like riflemen.

Indians watching from the woods saw a hundred or more heads bobbing up and down over the edge of a stockade wall.

Each of the thirty grown men in the garrison had several rifles in good working order, and many had shotguns. There were also some worn-out gun barrels which would never shoot again. So the Indians sometimes saw a couple of hundred gun barrels at one time.

That afternoon the Indians killed a few fat calves for meat but drove the other cattle up to the stockade so the settlers could milk as usual.

When Pompey appeared the next morning, with his flag of truce, Boone called to him that the whites had decided not to surrender.

Boone knew that the Indians would be very angry. He warned the settlers to get ready for trouble.

But hours passed, and no trouble came. Then the settlers had a surprise. Pompey returned with word that the Indians wanted peace. If the Kentuckians did not want to surrender, it might be possible to negotiate a peace treaty, he said. He suggested a conference for the next day and Boone agreed.

"Tomorrow," Boone said, "we must be careful. They have been honest with us so far, and they really thought we would surrender. But now they realize we have been tricking them to gain time. They may try some tricks of their own, and I can't say that I blame them. This offer is too good. They pretend to be more friendly than ever and that is a danger sign. We must keep our wits about us."

Next morning several tables were carried from the stockade and placed under a large sycamore tree within rifle shot of the stockade. Daniel and Squire Boone, Major Smith, Colonel Callaway, Flanders Callaway, and three other whites sat down at the tables to represent Boonesborough. Blackfish brought seventeen chiefs with him, one to represent each of the Shawnee villages. The Frenchman De Quindre was also there and he set up both a British and French flag, although it was well known that France was then helping the colonists against the British.

The Indian chiefs made long and dull speeches, but the Boonesborough men did not object. They wanted the conference to last as long as possible.

At noon the white men went into the stockade and brought out their best plates, knives, and forks, and an elaborate meal. They regretted losing all this food, because their supplies were very short, but they wanted the Indians to think they had plenty of everything to withstand a siege.

The peace delegates feasted. Then Boone and the other Boonesborough men carried the plates, knives, and forks and all leftovers back to the stockade.

In the afternoon the conference got down to drawing up the agreement itself. A clerk wrote down each clause when the delegates agreed upon it. The Ohio River was to be the boundary between the Shawnee and white nations. The two peoples were to live in friendship always.

Boone sometimes noticed Blackfish looking at him sadly, and he could guess what was going on in the old man's mind. Blackfish could not understand why a man like Boone, who had all the Indian virtues, could possibly want to live in this dreary log fort and plant corn and milk cows when he could live the life of a Shawnee chief.

But it was plain that Blackfish had made up his mind. If Boone insisted on living the white man's way, and if Boone would not keep a promise to his Shawnee brothers, then Blackfish could not show Boone any mercy.

Boone, on the other hand, was just as determined to fight the Indians, even though they had been kind to him. His people could not take up the Indian way, because they had been raised differently. They would be just as unhappy living in wigwams and dancing war dances as the Indians would be if they had to farm and live in log cabins.

Across the table, Boone and Blackfish watched each other suspiciously. The fact that they admired each other made no difference. They were enemies now, pretending to be friends while they planned war.

Late in the afternoon the agreement was completed and the "peace treaty" written. Blackfish said no treaty could be signed on the day it was written. Tomorrow morning they would meet again and go through the ceremony of peace.

Before leaving the stockade the next morning, Boone gave careful instructions. He placed his best riflemen along the wall overlooking the "peace conference."

"If we wave our hats," he said, "you open fire. Don't bother to take aim, but fire into the lump. We'll get back the best we can. Leave the gate open a little so we can run in, but not very far open."

He and the seven other delegates stacked their rifles just inside the gate and walked out to the final meeting.

Blackfish and seventeen other Shawnees marched from the forest to the big sycamore tree near the stockade.

Boone had a feeling that something was going to happen, but he did not know just what. He noticed that the Indian delegation was made up mostly of young warriors instead of the old chiefs who had come the day before.

"You have different chiefs today," he said to Blackfish.

"The same," Blackfish said.

The Indians carried no weapons except a peace pipe, but it was made in such a way that it was both a pipe and a tomahawk. Beneath the bowl was a blade.

The pipe was lighted and passed around, but it was passed only to Indians.

Blackfish arose and explained that to conclude a treaty of peace, the Shawnees not only shook hands. They touched breasts together, to indicate the meeting of hearts. Since there were eighteen Indians and only seven white delegates, each white man would shake hands with two Indians at the same time.

The seven whites lined up and the Indians faced them.

Inside the stockade, riflemen leveled their long guns.

One rifleman, stationed on a wall that did not overlook the sycamore tree, drew a bead on a young warrior who was sitting lazily on a stump in the clearing.

Boone now realized that when the delegates put their hearts together, two strong warriors would have holds on each white man. They were only a few steps from the bank of the river. Maybe the Indians intended to drag the white men over this bank.

No one knows exactly what either side intended to do at this moment, but we know what happened.

A shot rang out. White and Indian delegates began wrestling. Guns blazed from the stockade.

The white men ran for the fort. A bullet knocked Squire Boone down. It may have been a bullet from the stockade or from the nearby woods. But he got to his feet and ran to the gate.

Six of the delegates got through the gate, but the seventh was too late and had to flatten out behind a stump near the stockade wall and lie there.

A white man who wrote an account of this incident declares that the Indians tried to drag all seven of the white delegates to the river, and that Blackfish himself gave the signal which started the fighting.

If a Shawnee had written such an account, he would have said that the whites lured the eighteen Shawnee chiefs to the peace conference and tried to kill all of them by firing a surprise volley from the stockade wall.

Perhaps the white historian is correct, and the Shawnees really tried to capture the seven white delegates. But it seems that eighteen strong young warriors could have held fast to at least one or two of the whites.

Likewise, if white riflemen on the stockade wall had planned beforehand to shoot the Indian delegates, it seems that they would have killed some of them.

But the only man killed during this brief moment of confusion was the young warrior who was sunning himself on a stump far from the conference.

Why was he sitting there, an easy target, if the Indians planned to start the fight?

Probably the truth is that each side expected trouble at that moment. Rifles were cocked and aimed. Someone shouted or pulled a trigger, and the fight was on.

As soon as they got inside, Daniel and the five other delegates grabbed their rifles and began firing at clumps of bushes where Indians were hiding. Squire Boone had a bullet in his shoulder and was bleeding badly. He fired two shots and collapsed.

Daniel and another man carried him to his cabin. Daniel cut out the bullet and bandaged the wound. Squire was too weak to return to his place on the wall, but he asked them to leave an ax beside his bed. "When they break in," he said, "maybe I can get in a lick or two."

The seventh delegate was lying unhurt, behind a stump near the stockade wall. Bullets from the nearby woods kicked dirt on him and slapped against the stump. All day he lay, not daring to move, but when night came someone opened the gate slightly and he crawled to safety.

15

BULLETS AND FLAMING ARROWS

The Indians had plenty of ammunition and used it freely. Each of more than four hundred braves loaded and fired as fast as he could. The noise of their guns made a continuous roar all around the stockade, and the air became hazy with white smoke of burned powder. Bullets spatted against the logs and hissed through loopholes. The whites could only pop their heads up for an instant above the wall to see that no Indians were charging them.

The cattle had not been turned loose that morning, and when the firing began they stampeded around the enclosure, bawling with fright. Women and children screamed.

One Boonesborough man, a potter by trade, did not consider himself a fighter at all. He was there to make pots, not to kill Indians. When the battle began, he hid under the bellows in Squire Boone's blacksmith shop.

A women found him there and urged him out to do his duty. "I'm not made for a fighter," he said.

"Why don't you crawl down in the new well," she said. "The one we didn't finish. You'd be safer from bullets there. Take a shovel and dig. The deeper you are the safer you'll be."

He thought it was a good idea, and soon dirt was flying from the well.

A rail fence extended from the stockade out to the edge of the timber where the Indians were hiding. The Indians scattered flax along the fence and set it afire, and the flames crawled slowly along the fence toward the stockade.

The settlers hurriedly dug a tunnel under the wall of the stockade and up to the surface beneath the fence. They pulled the rails into the tunnel, while bullets crashed just over their heads. Thus they made a gap in the fence so the flames could not get to the wall.

The firing continued all day. When night came it lessened somewhat, but bullets still smacked against the walls steadily. The settlers got no sleep.

At dawn the firing ceased. The settlers peered over the walls. From the woods came the clear note of a bugle. Indians did not use bugles, so the settlers knew that the Frenchman De Quindre was tooting.

Daniel heard shouts in Shawnee.

"Some chief is ordering the warriors to gather the pack horses and prepare to march," he said.

"They're leaving!" the settlers cried. "They're retreating. It's all over."

"Don't let them fool you," Boone said. "If they were really leaving, the main body would move off quietly and about fifty would remain all day and keep up a steady firing."

The bugle note came again, this time from farther away.

"They hope we will open the gate and come out to

investigate. If we did, that would be the end of Boonesborough."

The settlers waited. The forest was quiet and peaceful. Birds chirped. But crows did not call calmly from tall trees.

In about an hour a warwhoop sounded and hundreds of rifles spoke in a ragged volley. It seemed a bucketful of bullets struck each loophole.

Some Indians were firing from a nearby hill. The range was very great, but by loading their rifles heavily and aiming at a high angle they could drop bullets into the stockade.

Several settlers were hit and some badly wounded, but few died of their wounds. A spent bullet struck Jemima Callaway in what a historian has called "the fleshy part of her back." The bullet carried the cloth of her skirt into the wound. She jerked the cloth and the bullet came out with the cloth. After that she limped but did not quit her work of caring for the wounded and loading rifles.

Squire Boone's old cow Spot was hit by one of these high-arching bullets, and for a while she was in a critical condition. But a settler cut the bullet out and she improved rapidly.

On the third day a watcher in a blockhouse noticed that the water of the Kentucky River was muddy at the point where the bank came nearest to the stockade. In a little while the muddy streak extended far downstream. It was plain that the Indians were digging a tunnel from the river bank toward the stockade and were throwing the dirt into the water.

The Frenchman De Quindre was teaching the Indians European methods of siege warfare. If the Indians kept digging, they could go right under the wall and walk into the stockade from underground.

There was only one thing to do. The settlers dug a very deep ditch inside the stockade and began their own tunnel. They threw fresh dirt over the stockade wall so the Indians would know what they were doing. They also constructed a watch tower of logs thick enough to stop bullets and set it on the roof of one of the corner blockhouses. From the tower, riflemen could see dirt being thrown into the river, but they could not see the warriors who were throwing it.

Suddenly well-aimed bullets began killing livestock in the center of the enclosure. Boone climbed into the watch tower and saw that a warrior had established himself in the top of a tree some 200 yards away.

Boone loaded his heaviest rifle and waited patiently. In a little while he saw the warrior's head among the leaves. He took careful aim and fired. The warrior pitched headlong to the ground.

It was the Negro Pompey, who had been born a slave of the whites, had escaped and become an important member of the Shawnee tribe. Now he had died in battle, fighting for his adopted people.

Meanwhile Squire Boone had an idea. Lying in his cabin, he listened to bullets whacking against the logs a foot from his ear and thought how fortunate he was that these bullets were not cannon balls. He eyed the ax lying on his table and planned how he would swing it with his one good arm if the Indians swarmed into the place. Then he daydreamed of peaceful times when he had cut wood with this ax.

He remembered that there was a big black gum log

near his blacksmith shop. A black gum log cannot be split. To work it into firewood you have to saw it into short blocks and cut off slabs. Gum is one of the toughest and most contrary kinds of wood.

He sat up in bed with his grand idea. Why not make a cannon from this tough log? He began planning how this could be done.

About the fourth day of the siege he was able to get up and begin work with one hand. He and a helper heated irons and burned out the center of the log, then they heated wagon tires and wrapped them around it to make it stronger. Finally they mounted it on a swivel.

Squire put more than a pound of powder in his wooden cannon, plenty of wadding, about thirty 1-ounce rifle balls and perhaps a few scraps of iron which he found about the place.

One patch of bushes near the fort was always full of Indians. On a foggy morning the settlers hoisted the cannon to the top of the stockade wall and aimed it at the bushes. All the men except Squire backed off to a safe distance. Women and children held their ears.

Squire put the red-hot end of a rod to the touchhole. There was a roar which shook the stockade and started the cattle stampeding again.

As the great cloud of white smoke lifted, the settlers saw a dozen Indians sprinting from the bushes toward the woods. The settlers sent up a great cheer.

One of them later wrote that "the Indians squandered from that place much frightened. It made them skamper perdidiously whether they was hit with the bullets or whether it was the big loud report was uncertain." Anyway the settlers enjoyed seeing them run.

Squire and his helpers lowered the cannon and poured water into it to put out the fire in the wood which the powder had started. When it had dried a little, Squire loaded it again and the settlers aimed it at another patch of Indians.

Squire was excited. With this mighty cannon they

Squire touched off the wooden cannon

could comb the Indians out of every patch of weeds and bushes within rifle range of the stockade.

The others had confidence in the cannon now and stood closer.

Squire touched it off. Another roar. Men standing nearest were knocked down. The gun had burst at the breech and was a tangled mass of kindling wood and wagon tires. Squire picked himself up, brushed the splinters out of his hair and remarked that now at least it would not be much trouble to work the log up into firewood.

The siege had continued longer than anyone expected. Indians did not like siege operations. Sitting around behind stumps and firing at a log wall was not their idea of fighting. Always before in Kentucky they had retired after a couple of days.

Boone knew that the Frenchman De Quindre was the answer to this riddle. He had persuaded the Indians to remain and dig the tunnel, promising them that Boonesborough would surrender as soon as the tunnel reached the wall.

The settlers were much worried about the tunnel but even more concerned over their water supply. They were all parched with thirst. They had saved a little water to use if the Indians set the stockade afire, but they knew they would soon have to drink it all just to keep alive.

Some of them said that the Indians would not have the courage to rush through the tunnel, once it was completed.

Boone told them they were wrong. When only a thin wall of earth remained between the Indians' tunnel and the white men's ditch, plenty of Indians would volunteer to push through, even though it meant almost certain death for the first ones.

It was Boone's hope that the Indians would not finish their tunnel. He explained that digging in the ground was considered disgraceful work for a warrior. He could guess how much trouble De Quindre was having in persuading the Indians to continue the disgusting work. "They think it will make women out of them. Our best chance is that they will quit work before they dig far enough."

But even this hope began to fade when on the seventh day the settlers in their own ditch could hear the click of shovels as the Indians dug toward them. The braves had only a few more yards to dig and a few more tons of earth to throw into the river.

It was a gloomy day but no rain had fallen. A flaming arrow came from the bushes, arched high into the air and fell on a cabin roof. A settler climbed up and beat out the flames with a broom while bullets whizzed around him.

A fire arrow struck another roof and men from inside the cabin managed to break through the roof, knocking the shingles upward with their gun barrels. Many other arrows came, but most hit the ground inside the enclosure where they did no damage.

Some of these arrows were wrapped in the inner bark of shellbark hickory which burns fiercely. Others were cylinders filled with powder, like firecrackers, and were ignited by a piece of punk which served as a fuse. They exploded after they landed.

Late in the day scores of these arrows arched into the stockade, and sometimes three or four fires started at the same time. Men, women, and boys beat out the flames.

Squire Boone was working furiously in his blacksmith shop, making a piston to fit in an old rifle barrel. When someone asked him what he was doing, he explained he was making a squirtgun. It seemed he had gone out of his mind, to be making a toy at such a time. But when he had finished his squirtgun, he put out a blaze using only about a pint of water, and the settlers admitted that he had a good idea.

As thick darkness settled, the attack increased in fury.

Suddenly several warriors rushed toward the stockade carrying lighted torches. The defenders fired but could not stop all of them. Some managed to fling their torches against the stockade wall.

One torch fell against the outer door of a cabin, and soon the door was blazing to the top. John Holder, Fanny Callaway's husband, pushed the door open, ran outside, and threw a bucket of water on the flames. A dozen rifles cracked in the bushes. When he got back inside and bolted the door, he found several bullet holes through his clothing. But he had not been hit.

"If they can get one good blaze going," Daniel Boone said, "they will push through the tunnel and at the same time charge the walls from all sides."

One Boonesborough man, William Patton, had been away from home on a long hunt and did not know of the Indian attack. As he neared home, on this seventh night of the siege, he saw the stockade blazing, heard the rattle of rifle fire and whoops of Indians and screams of women.

He ran for Logan's Station and informed the settlers there that the Indians had captured Boonesborough and scalped the garrison.

He was wrong. The Boonesborough people, with brooms and Squire's squirtgun, managed to put out every blaze before the walls were seriously damaged. Toward morning a drizzling rain began to fall. The Indians continued their fire attack, but cabin roofs burned more slowly. Finally, when the settlers were dropping from weariness, a heavy rain began to fall.

They caught rainwater in buckets and drank their fill. Then the women and children huddled in those cabins which still had roofs and went to sleep. Men dozed at their posts.

All the next day the rain came in torrents. Rifles cracked from the woods, when a man looked over the stockade wall, so they knew the Indians were still there.

When night came the rain slackened, but the sky did not clear. Indians might be creeping up ready to leap over the walls. The men were now so tired that they fell asleep standing up.

At dawn everyone was awakened by a shout. A man in the watch tower was pointing toward the river.

"Look what happened!" he called.

Men and women leaped up, ran to the wall, and looked over.

A deep pit extended from the river bank almost to the wall. Because of the heavy rain, the roof of the tunnel had fallen in.

"That's the end," Daniel said. "They won't try any more."

He was right. At sunup he and others went out and looked around. The Indians were gone.

About each loophole in the stockade walls there was a thick crust of lead, where bullets had lodged in the wood and flattened out, one on top of the other. The settlers that day gathered 125 pounds of lead from the walls and the ground nearby.

16

A THIEF UNDER THE BED

After people have faced death together, dressed each other's wounds, shared the last gourd of water and handful of parched corn, looked upon each other with boundless love and sympathy, and then together achieved a great victory—after all this they begin quarreling.

Pressed together by the enemy, they fly apart when the pressure is removed.

On the first day after the siege was lifted, the people of Boonesborough had plenty of energy. They were so glad to be alive that they thought little of their ruined crops or their other losses.

But there is nothing like a good night's sleep to bring out deep-seated weariness. The next day they were sunk in gloom. Several of their best cows had been killed inside the stockade. The Indians had killed all game within ten miles. They had plenty of lead but little powder.

They began to hate each other. Women scolded and men snarled over trifles. Boone never quarreled. When he was irritated by someone, he kept his temper and avoided the person as best he could. But now, to his great disgust, he found himself the center of a lively and unpleasant controversy.

His old friend Colonel Callaway suddenly turned on him and said that he, Daniel Boone, was the cause of all their troubles.

Callaway declared that Daniel had betrayed the men at the salt camp and helped the Shawnees capture them.

Daniel wearily pointed out that the Indians themselves had found the camp and would have killed all the men if Daniel hadn't talked them out of it.

"You joined the Shawnee tribe and plotted with them to destroy this settlement," Callaway roared.

"Why did I escape from them and come back here?" Daniel asked.

"That was part of the scheme—"

"Why did I stay here and help you fight them off, when I wanted to go back to North Carolina and see my family? Why did I risk my scalp—"

"You planned to turn us all over to the British—"

Flanders Callaway, the colonel's nephew and Daniel's son-in-law, sided with Daniel. So did most of the other Boonesborough people. But the colonel continued to roar. He probably would have roared himself out in a few days and the whole matter would have been forgotten, but Daniel insisted on a public hearing.

Most of the men at the three Kentucky settlements belonged to the Kentucky militia. Daniel was a captain in that organization. He said that this argument was a militia matter, and he demanded a trial before a regular court-martial.

Officers of the militia were called in from Logan's Station and Harrodsburg and a trial was held. Colonel Callaway repeated his charges and demanded that Boone's commission be taken from him.

Boone told his story. The court-martial immediately declared he was not guilty. Soon after that Boone was promoted from captain to major.

About the time this argument was settled, reinforcements arrived from Virginia. Boonesborough was safe at last. Daniel Boone saddled a horse and rode down the Wilderness trail toward North Carolina. He was taking a vacation from the hard job of fighting Indians and conquering the wilderness.

No one knows exactly what he did during the following twelve months. He found Rebecca and the children safe and well, living in a small cabin on a farm belonging to her relatives. Certainly Daniel had some fascinating tales to tell, when the family and neighbors gathered around the fireplace on a long winter evening.

Meanwhile, important events were happening west of the mountains. A small army of Virginians under George Rogers Clark pushed into the "northwest," as the country north of Kentucky was then called, and captured three British forts. Without these forts the British found it much more difficult to agitate among the Indians.

In the spring of 1779, while Daniel was in North Carolina, about two hundred men from the Kentucky settlements, under a Colonel Bowman, marched into Indian country and attacked Chillicothe.

The Indians were not expecting this attack. Blackfish with a party of warriors had just left town. When the whites began to fire into Chillicothe, only twenty-five warriors and fifteen boys were there to defend it. Women and children huddled in the council house while the warriors and boys fired at the attackers. A messenger got through the lines and told Blackfish what was happening.

Blackfish was badly wounded

Blackfish and his party returned and charged through the white lines. Blackfish was badly wounded in the leg. As the fight continued, some Indians suggested that they surrender, in the hope that the white men would have some magic medicine which would save Blackfish's life. But the old chief refused to surrender. After a few hours of fighting, the whites withdrew.

Blackfish died several weeks later.

In the fall of 1779, Daniel Boone, two of his younger brothers, and a dozen other farmers, each with a large family, started for Kentucky. One of these farmers was Abraham Lincoln. His grandson, born thirty years later in Kentucky, became the sixteenth president of the United States.

Some of Daniel's neighbors, who did not go on the trip, took up a collection and bought him two cannon, called "swivel guns."

Because the trail had been widened, it was now possible to make the trip in wagons. Each family had one or more covered wagons. A man who saw the wagon train depart said it was a half-mile long and looked more like an army than a party of settlers.

Before they had gone far, some of the horses died. Daniel discovered that in order to ford the Cumberland River he would have to throw away either some provisions or the cannon. He knew they would need these big guns when the Indians attacked, but he was more afraid of hunger during the coming winter than he was of Indians. He left the guns beside the river, hoping someday to send a party back to get them. They were made of bronze and would not rust. But he never sent for them. There was always too much to do in Kentucky.

The wagon train did not stop at Boonesborough, probably because Daniel did not want to live too near his one-time friend, Colonel Callaway. Instead, Daniel started a new settlement, called Boone's Station, a few miles north.

Soon other wagon trains crawled past Boone's Station, and several settlements were established between the Licking and Kentucky rivers, north of Boone's Station. Kentucky was booming again.

For a few months at least, the new settlers did not have to fear Indian attacks. George Rogers Clark and his Virginians had built a fort at the falls of the Ohio, northwest of the Kentucky settlements, and were prepared to move against any large Indian army that crossed the Ohio.

But the settlers that winter had two other enemies as dangerous as Indians—cold and hunger. Winter came early. Layers of ice covered the trees and grass. Snow piled up in the hollows so that wagons could not travel. Cattle and hogs froze to death.

Food supplies that the newcomers had brought from the east in their covered wagons were soon eaten up. The price of corn went to sixty dollars a bushel. Then nobody had even a bushel. When the people at Boone's Station divided their last piece of corn bread, they listened to the wind howling outside their cabins and wondered if they would be alive when spring came.

Daniel and the other men hunted every day, even during blizzards, but usually came home with nothing. Once in a while they killed a deer or buffalo, but the meat was lean and tough because the animals themselves were at the point of starvation. More often they found carcasses of animals that had frozen to death.

Perhaps many of the newcomers, as they huddled in their cabins, half-starved and blue with cold, wished they had never left their comfortable homes in North Carolina. But before anyone actually starved, honks sounded from the gray sky, and fat geese and ducks settled on pools in the woods. Men loaded their guns and hid in the canebrakes. Soon everyone was eating roast goose and duck, and Kentucky was once again a wonderful place.

Now men began worrying about titles to the land they had staked out. To get a clear title to a piece of land, it was necessary to pay a certain sum of money to the Virginia government. The settlers had money. The problem was how to send it to Virginia.

Daniel was the man they trusted most, and they insisted that he take their money to Virginia. It was not the sort of job he liked, but he had no choice. With between forty and fifty thousand dollars in his saddlebag, he started east with one companion.

Daniel Boone could outwit honest Indians in the woods, but he was no match for dishonest whites. He and his companion got safely through the mountains, but as they neared the end of their journey they stopped at an inn in James City, Virginia. Here they ate a big meal, went to their room and carefully locked the door. They did not look under the bed. Daniel put the saddlebag beside the bed.

Daniel must have known in the back of his mind that he had not taken proper precautions, that he was somehow being careless, for that night he dreamed that his father, who had been dead for about 15 years, was frowning at him.

At that time it was widely believed that the dead had a special knowledge of the future and could appear to the living in dreams and warn them of trouble ahead. Although Daniel was not superstitious, compared with most people of that period, he believed that his father sometimes came to him this way and warned him of disaster.

The next morning he awoke, dizzy and bewildered. Evidently he and his companion had been drugged.

His papers were scattered about the room. The door was open. The saddlebag and some of his clothes were missing.

He shook his companion awake and the two, half-dressed, began a search. They found the saddlebag at the foot of the stairs, empty. The missing garments had been thrown out the window into the garden.

They searched the inn from cellar to attic and found a little of the paper money in some jugs in the cellar.

Daniel believed that the landlord had planned the robbery, and an old woman who worked at the inn had hid under the bed before they entered the room the night before. But he could prove nothing.

He returned sorrowfully to Kentucky. Every cent of his own money had been in the saddlebag, along with the funds of other settlers, so he could not pay back the money he had lost.

Few of the settlers blamed him. Some told him to forget about the money. In later years he was able to pay others in land for the money which had been stolen from him.

17

RIFLE SHOTS IN THE WOODS

Daniel Boone and Colonel Callaway would probably have patched up their differences and become friends again if they had had a chance. Daniel was not one to hold a grudge. Callaway, although sometimes angry and blustering, was honest and well meaning. Other members of the Boone and Callaway families remained good friends. Undoubtedly, Daniel's daughter, Jemima Callaway, would have brought Daniel and the Colonel together eventually, but she never had the opportunity.

In March, 1780, about the time that Daniel was being robbed in Virginia, Colonel Callaway and another man were killed and scalped by the Indians about a mile and a half from Boonesborough. The same day a third man was killed in the nearby woods. Within a week Squire Boone and several other men were wounded. It was plain that British agents were again busy among the Indians.

In June several hundred Indians and a few British soldiers raided Kentucky. They brought two cannon with them and with these big guns they easily demolished two new stockades near Blue Licks, north of Boone's Station. The Indians killed some of the captives taken on this raid but permitted the British to take most of them to Detroit.

In retaliation, George Rogers Clark and his soldiers from Virginia left their fort at the Falls of the Ohio, collected a force of Kentucky riflemen, and invaded the Shawnee country.

Daniel Boone had returned from Virginia meanwhile, and he commanded a detachment from Boone's Station and Boonesborough on this raid. The Virginians and Kentuckians burned Chillicothe and other Indian towns. Some of Clark's soldiers got out of hand and killed several captives, including a woman.

The Kentuckians hoped that their raid would teach the Indians to keep out of Kentucky, but they were wrong.

One night Daniel and twenty-five of his men, on a hunting trip, camped in the woods south of the Kentucky River. While the others were relaxing after supper, Daniel heard something which made him uneasy. Perhaps a nightbird somewhere off in the woods called out in surprise, or perhaps there was silence where there should have been noise. He did not explain but slipped away from the group.

Soon he was back. "They're all around us," he said. "Roll up some blankets so they will look like men asleep."

He gathered an armful of twigs and put them on the fire in such a way that they would smolder for a while and then blaze up briefly. "Before this wood catches fire," he said, "we'll crawl off into the bushes."

The men followed his instructions. When the fire blazed up, Indians hidden a few hundred yards away saw what looked like men sleeping peacefully. Then the fire died down. Hours passed and nothing happened. Probably some of the men wondered if Daniel's imagination had got the better of him.

With the first light of dawn, rifles cracked and bullets went through blanket rolls. There was a warwhoop. Indians charged toward the camp site. The whites opened fire. The Indians fell on their faces and crawled away, dragging their wounded with them.

On another occasion Daniel was hunting alone near Blue Licks. Beside a little stream called Slate Creek he saw Indian signs, probably moccasin prints.

He got out of sight and cautiously followed the trail for several miles. Approaching a small spring, he listened and watched for a while, then crept forward and took a drink. A shot sounded nearby and a bullet knocked the bark from a tree trunk just above his head. He leaped up, ran to a thicket, and from there worked his way to a canebrake beside the creek. Here he hid and waited.

There was a stir in the bushes on the hillside and two brown heads appeared. If Daniel shot one of them, the other would shoot him before he could reload. If he ran, they would chase him and could probably keep between him and the nearest white settlement. The canebrake was small.

He knew they were good woodsmen because they had already outwitted him, hiding so well that he came within shooting range without seeing them. His only advantage lay in marksmanship. He could save his scalp only by luck and a careful shot.

As they crept toward him he drew a bead on the head of the first one and waited. The second raised himself to have a look. Daniel pulled the trigger. His bullet went through the head of the first and struck the second in the shoulder, knocking him down. The second dropped his gun and ran.

Daniel examined their rifles, kept the better one and threw the other in the creek.

In October, 1780, Daniel and his brother Edward, some ten years younger, went on horseback to Blue Licks to make salt. On their return journey they halted beneath a hickory tree to crack nuts and let their horses graze.

Daniel saw a bear almost out of shooting range. Game was scarce and the settlement needed meat, so Daniel fired. The bear lumbered off, but Daniel knew it was wounded and would soon drop dead. He ran after it, neglecting to reload. Just as he found the carcass, he heard shots behind him, then the baying of a hound.

He knew that Edward was either dead or a prisoner and nothing could be done for him.

Daniel started reloading just as the hound came in sight. Knowing that the Indians would be close behind the dog, he sprinted for a nearby canebrake. His ramrod slipped out of his hand as he ran and he could not stop to pick it up.

He reached the canebrake before the Indians caught sight of him, but he knew he could not hide if the dog kept on his trail. When it came close to him, he made threatening gestures and it ran back toward its Indian masters. But soon it took up the trail again.

Daniel broke off a slender stalk of cane to use as a ramrod and finished reloading. When the dog came in sight again he shot it.

Later he heard the Indians whooping with anger when they found the body of the dog, but they did not pursue him farther.

Daniel went back to the settlement, and the next day led a party to the place. They found Edward's body and trailed the Indians as far as the Ohio. On the way back they stopped to hunt, for in Kentucky in those days little

They found Edward's body

time could be spared to mourn the dead. The living must have food.

Kentucky was then a part of Virginia, and the settlers elected Daniel as one of their representatives in the Virginia State Assembly. In April of the following year, 1781, he was attending a session of the Assembly at Charlottesville, Virginia, when a force of 250 British dragoons galloped into town.

The legislators ran into the woods and hid, except

Daniel and a few others who remained to load some official papers in a wagon. After this chore was done, Daniel and a man named Jouett mounted their horses and rode calmly along a street. Parties of dragoons dashed past them, looking for members of the Assembly.

"If the redcoats stop us," Daniel said, "just act like you don't expect them to arrest us, and they probably won't. Redcoats are like Indians. They treat you like you expect to be treated, I think."

Daniel was dressed frontier style, in a buckskin hunting shirt, trousers and leggings which had seen much wear, and he did not look at all like a member of the Assembly or a high officer in the Kentucky militia. Moreover he was talking so calmly to Jouett that the dragoons could tell he was not excited.

But when he and Jouett walked their horses out of town, a squad of dragoons galloped up to them and began asking questions.

Daniel said they were on their way home. He asked them how the war was going, in a tone which indicated he did not care how it was going.

The dragoons rode along beside them, trying to make up their minds about these country characters. Daniel bored them with some talk about his troubles out on the farm. The sergeant in command of the squad began to lose interest.

They came to a crossroad and Jouett said to Daniel, "Well, Colonel, this is our road."

"Colonel!" shouted the sergeant. "You are just such prisoners as we want."

The dragoons took the two men back to town and locked them up.

But Daniel was not easy to keep, as the Shawnee Indians had already discovered. No one knows how or when he escaped from the British, but in August he was back in Kentucky. In September he visited his boyhood home in Pennsylvania, where some of his relatives still lived. From November until January, 1782, he again served as a member of the Virginia Assembly.

Daniel Boone did not like to orate or listen to others orate. Making laws was to him like raising corn. Perhaps it was necessary, but very dull. In December the Assembly ordered its sergeant-at-arms to find Daniel Boone and see that he attended more regularly. Daniel had slipped off to do a little hunting in the Virginia woods.

The Revolutionary War was now over, although peace had not been declared. But the British still hoped to keep the land west of the mountains. For Kentucky, the year 1782 was "the year of blood."

18

THE BATTLE OF BLUE LICKS

The British at Detroit continued to agitate the Shawnees, long after Cornwallis surrendered to Washington at Yorktown. Raids and massacres continued along the Pennsylvania and Virginia frontiers. One side was as bloodthirsty as the other.

Many Indians still lived east of the mountains. They had adopted "the white man's way" and had no quarrel with anybody. A mob of white men attacked one village of unarmed Indian farmers and murdered ninety-six men, women, and children.

The British told the Shawnees of this massacre and warned them that the same thing would happen to them if they ever made peace with the Long Knives.

Soon after that, in June, 1782, about five hundred Pennsylvanians and Virginians invaded Shawnee territory. The Shawnees defeated them in a battle on the Sandusky River in Ohio and burned their commander at the stake.

The fierce Wyandot Indians lived west of Kentucky. They had always been enemies of the Shawnees, but when they heard that the whites had killed unresisting Indians in the East, they made peace with the Shawnees and sent war parties into Kentucky.

When Daniel Boone returned to Kentucky in the spring, he found that the settlers were expecting an attack by a large force of Shawnees or Wyandots or both but did not know when or where the attack would be made.

One morning early in August, the settlers at a new stockade, called Bryan's Station, discovered that their hundred-acre cornfield was full of Indians. No one knows how they discovered this, for the Indians were well hidden. Perhaps the dogs barked in a peculiar way, or someone saw corntassles sway when no breeze was blowing.

Plainly the Indians were waiting for the whites to open the gates and go out to work. The whites kept the gates closed. There was no well inside the stockade and the water buckets were empty. If flaming arrows set the cabins afire, they could not fight the flames. The weather was hot, and they would soon suffer from thirst.

Now the women had an idea. "Let us go out to the spring, carrying buckets as we always do, and laughing and talking. The Indians will be sure that we do not know they are there. They will wait for you men to come out before they begin shooting."

At first the men objected. It was too dangerous, they said. "What if the Indians start scalping you!"

But the women argued. If they didn't get water, the stockade would burn down and they would all be scalped anyway. This was their only chance. Finally the men agreed.

The women opened the gate slightly and went out with their buckets, talking in lively fashion. In groups of three or four they walked to the spring, a short distance from the stockade, and filled their buckets. Some made a second trip.

Two men mounted horses and rode out of the gate at a walk, talking lazily to each other, pretending they were going out to work and were in no hurry.

When all the women had returned with their buckets and the two horsemen were out of sight, the settlers pulled the gate shut.

The Indians waited until the sun came up. There was not a sound to disturb the peace of the August morning. When the Indians realized at last that the whites knew they were there, they decided to pull a trick to draw the white men outside.

About a dozen Indians walked toward the back side of the stockade, making no pretense of keeping out of sight. They hoped that most of the white men would come out of the back gate and chase them, thus leaving the front side of the stockade undefended.

But the whites knew this trick also. Twenty-five of the best riflemen, each with two or three loaded rifles beside him, remained on the front side. Ten or twelve men ran out the back gate to chase Indians, or rather to pretend to chase them. They fired rifles and shouted, making as much noise as they could. This was double trickery.

A hundred or more Indians charged the front. The riflemen there had a good target. They fired. Dozens of Indians fell, and the others ran back to shelter.

All day long the Indians continued to fire on the stockade, but only two settlers were killed. Fire arrows ignited some cabin roofs, but the settlers put out the flames before much damage was done. One flaming arrow landed in the cradle of a baby named Richard Mentor Johnson, but the baby was unhurt, and grew up to become the ninth Vice-President of the United States.

Meanwhile the two horsemen, who rode out so lazily that morning, had galloped to a nearby settlement and spread the alarm. In the afternoon a party of sixteen horsemen and thirty riflemen came to relieve the besieged stockade. The horsemen charged straight through the Indian lines and reached the stockade without any losses. The thirty men on foot got into the cornfield and fought a battle but had to retire after two of them were killed.

The Indians knew that more whites would soon arrive, so they slipped away and marched north toward Blue Licks.

Early the next morning Daniel Boone arrived with a detachment of men from Boonesborough and Boone's Station.

Dead cattle, sheep, and hogs lay bloating in the sun. All buildings outside the stockade had been burned. A field of hemp was ruined. Potato vines had been pulled up. Every stalk in the big cornfield had been broken or stripped of its leaves. The Indians had worked hard to destroy the property of the whites.

This was war. Whites had often destroyed villages and crops of the Indians.

Inside the stockade, two women sat staring grimly into space, mourning their dead husbands. Men were silent and angry.

Soon detachments from two other settlements arrived. A little less than two hundred fighting men were now present. Most of them wanted to follow the Indians immediately, although the Indians supposedly numbered three or four hundred.

An officer in one detachment, Major Hugh McGary, pointed out that four or five hundred more men would arrive next day from the settlements farther south. He suggested that they wait for reinforcements.

Colonel John Todd, commander of that detachment, ridiculed McGary, hinting that McGary was afraid. Todd said if they waited another day the Indians would get safely across the Ohio. Daniel Boone, who now held the rank of lieutenant colonel, kept still.

The men were in a fighting mood, and almost all of them agreed with Todd. At noon they took up the trail.

Daniel was worried. The men were too angry to have good judgment. Like all frontier fighters, they lacked discipline. They obeyed a command if they felt like it. Officers were only advisors. Daniel knew how dangerous it was for a crowd—they could not be called an army—of angry whites to engage a band of well-disciplined Indians, especially when the Indians greatly outnumbered the whites.

Daniel was also worried about his son Israel, now twenty-three years old, who had insisted on coming along although he had a fever. Israel had a strong constitution, but fever can strike down the strongest man.

Daniel studied the trail the Indians had left and did not like what he saw. The Indians were moving slowly and blazing the trail as they went, so the Kentuckians could follow easily.

"They're stepping in each other's tracks," he pointed out, "so we won't know how many they are. They want to fight."

The men marched all afternoon and most of the night. Next morning they came to the Licking River at Blue Licks. Here the river made a horseshoe bend around a big bare hill.

Colonel Todd asked Daniel's opinion.

Daniel pointed to the hill across the river.

"Just behind the bare hill," he said, "are two ravines. I'm sure the Indians are hiding there. They hope we will cross here and march up the hill. Then they will have us trapped, with the river on three sides. We'd better wait for reinforcements."

There was an angry murmur among the men. McGary had been accused of cowardice for making the same suggestion the day before. They made it plain that they were not going to wait.

"If you're bound to fight now," Boone said, "most of us should go upstream to Elk Creek, where there's a good ford, and cross there, without any noise and get in position to attack from the flank. Then a few should cross here, making a lot of noise, and we'll hit them on the side when they're looking this way."

"That'll take half a day," one of the men growled.

McGary had been in a sulk ever since he had been accused of cowardice. He wanted to prove he was no coward. He made a sneering remark about people who were afraid of Indians.

Boone was angered but he did not show it. "If you want to fight at a disadvantage," he said, "go ahead. I can go as far into an Indian fight as any other man."

"What did we come here for?" McGary yelled at the men.

"To fight Indians," they answered.

"By Godly, let's fight 'em. All who are not damned cowards follow me!" He slapped his horse with the reins and rode into the river.

Most of the men followed in a disorderly crowd. Boone, Todd, and the leader of the third detachment, Stephen Trigg, were left alone.

"We've got to go with them and get them into some kind of order," Boone said.

The three commanders forded the river and formed their men into thin battle lines. Trigg took the right, Todd the center, and Boone the left. All the men dismounted and left their horses standing, reins down, near the river, except McGary and about twenty-five others who were in a hurry to fight.

They walked to the top of the hill and started down the other side toward the ravines. McGary whooped and he and the other mounted men charged toward the thicket.

The bushes spurted flame and white smoke, and the ground shook with the roar of hundreds of rifles. Men and horses went down in a tangled mass as the smoke cloud rolled over them.

Boone and his men charged toward the ravine ahead of them, crouching as they ran. The Indians at this end of the line fired too soon, and only a few of Boone's men were hit. The others leaped into the ravine with their rifles still loaded, and a desperate game of hide-and-seek began.

Many of the Indians ran for their lives. Others tried to remain hidden as they reloaded. Daniel that day was carrying not his usual rifle but a fowling piece—a large shotgun—loaded with three or four balls and a dozen buckshot.

He knew that an Indian was hiding somewhere near him. His rule was never look for an Indian, because you can't see him. Look for his gun, which he can't hide.

Daniel watched until he saw a long rifle barrel being cautiously leveled in his direction.

"You be there!" he shouted and pulled the trigger of his fowling piece.

Knowing that at least some of his buckshot had found their mark, he stood up cautiously to see if any other Indians remained in the ravine. All was clear. His men had won this end of the battle.

Behind him he heard a shout. McGary rode up.

"Colonel Boone," he yelled. "Retreat. They broke our lines."

Boone climbed out of the ravine and looked around. The battle had been going on only about five minutes, but only a few of Todd's and Trigg's men were still alive, and they were racing toward the river.

Boone gathered his men and began a retreat. A force of Indians charged them but were stopped by a volley. A riderless horse trotted past. Daniel caught the horse and ordered his sick son, Israel, to mount and ride for the river.

"I won't leave you," Israel said. "I'm all right."

Daniel reloaded his gun.

A shot came from a nearby thicket and Israel fell. Daniel picked him up. An Indian with a tomahawk ran toward them. Daniel dropped Israel and shot the Indian.

When he picked Israel up again, he saw that the boy was dead.

He carried the body toward the river, but he knew he could not get across with it. There was a cave nearby where he had once camped. He hid the body there.

Then he caught a horse and rode after his men. He managed to get most of them safely across the river.

A few men from the other detachments also got across, including McGary who was largely responsible for the defeat. The Indians did not attempt to follow them far on their retreat.

During the rest of his long life, Daniel Boone blamed himself for the defeat at Blue Licks. He felt he should have thought of some way to make the men listen to him. He should have brought them to their senses somehow.

No one else blamed him. "This wouldn't have happened if we had done what Colonel Boone told us to do," they said.

19

THE NEW START

The battle of Blue Licks was the last pitched battle of the Revolution. The Thirteen Colonies had won their independence, and the settlers in Kentucky had won the fight for the new land, although they did not know it for many months.

Immediately after the battle, the Indian danger seemed greater than ever. An army of settlers went into the Ohio country and burned Indian towns, but they did not feel any safer after they returned. One settler offered to trade fourteen hundred acres of land for one horse to take him back to Virginia.

But to everyone's surprise, there were no attacks that winter. The following summer, 1783, a man rode into Boone's Station with a big piece of paper stuck in his cap. On the paper was written the word "Peace." He brought news that a peace treaty had been signed between Britain and the American states.

Small bands of Indians came to Kentucky that summer, ambushed and scalped settlers, destroyed crops and took horses, but to Daniel Boone and other old Indian fighters, such raids seemed tame. Daniel and Rebecca built a cabin three miles west of the stockade and settled there for what they hoped would be a quiet life of farming.

For a while their life was quiet, perhaps too quiet to suit Daniel. He planted a patch of tobacco and built a shed for drying the stalks. Daniel did not use tobacco, but it was a good cash crop.

The shed was tall and had cross beams at three levels, one above the other. Daniel's first crop filled the shed from top to bottom. One day after the stalks were dry and about ready to take to market, he climbed up to inspect the stalks on the upper level. He was careful not to shake them. A dry stalk of tobacco is covered with a fine dust. If you get this dust in your eyes, you are blinded for a while, and if you breathe it you start sneezing and coughing.

Daniel was standing on a beam, when he heard a noise and looked down to see several Shawnee warriors in the shed, with their rifles pointed at him.

"How d' do!" he exclaimed.

"Boone," they said, "this time we got you. You won't get away. You come with us to Chillicothe."

Boone knew some of them. He seemed glad to see them. He asked about their families.

"Come down," they ordered.

Boone was unarmed. If he did not come down, they could shoot him, scalp him, and escape without difficulty. If he surrendered, they could take him and Rebecca and the children north, and the neighbors would probably never know what happened to the Boone family.

Daniel said he would climb down in a minute, but first he wanted to pick out his best stalk of tobacco to give his Shawnee friends.

He lifted a stalk carefully from its peg. The Indians were looking up at him, eyes and mouths open.

A cloud of brown dust filled the air

He held his breath, squinted his eyes almost shut and shook the dusty stalk in the upturned faces. He kicked a beam with all his strength, and the force of his kick shook the whole shed. A cloud of brown dust filled the air.

Daniel leaped from his perch to the floor of the shed and ran out the door. The Indians yelled, coughed, sneezed, wept, and felt their way out of the shed. Gasping for breath and trying to get the tears out of their eyes, they trotted toward the woods, for they knew that Daniel was safe in his cabin and would soon have a big fowling piece, loaded with buckshot, aimed at them.

But except for these few minutes of excitement, farm life was very dull. Daniel and Rebecca moved to a newly built town on the Ohio River. Daniel became a trader, surveyor, and real estate dealer. He was elected a member of the legislature. But business and politics were as dull as farming.

Sometimes he was rich. Usually he was poor. Men cheated him in land deals. He became hopelessly entangled in lawsuits. He forgot to file claims to land. He was no match for shrewd land speculators who flocked into Kentucky.

For years Daniel tried to make himself over into a businessman and politician, but it was no use. He and Rebecca moved from place to place, but they were never happy except when they went on camping trips far from the settlements.

Once a traveler came upon the Boones in the hills of eastern Kentucky. Daniel and Rebecca, with two of their daughters and the daughters' husbands, were living in the woods in a "half-faced" camp. They ate from a wooden trough, using forks made of cane stalks. Here Daniel was happy. He had just killed a bear which measured two feet across the hips. The camp was stocked with salted bear meat and skins.

But Daniel could not afford to go on trips like this very often. A man could no longer make a living by hunting alone. He began thinking of the far west, where there was still "elbow room."

In 1795, Daniel's youngest son, Daniel Morgan Boone, went on a long hunting and exploring trip to the Mississippi River, into the land then owned by Spain. He returned with glowing accounts. Daniel made plans.

In 1799, when he was nearly sixty-five, Daniel cut down a large tulip poplar tree on the bank of a stream which flows into the Ohio. From the trunk he made a dugout canoe sixty feet long, capable of carrying five tons.

Daniel's brother Squire, and Daniel's two sons, Daniel Morgan and Nathan, also made big canoes. Neighbors heard that the Boones were going west, and several other families made boats.

Household goods were loaded into the canoes and flat-bottomed boats.

In September the flotilla started. Rebecca, her daughter Jemima Callaway and other women and most of the men went in the boats. Daniel and his son-in-law Flanders Callaway drove a herd of livestock along the bank. They were going west to begin life anew, where the hunting was still good.

20

ELBOW ROOM

The next twenty years were to Daniel the most satisfactory years of his life. Few men have lived so vigorously and fully after the age of sixty-five.

Often he was irritated, disappointed. Sometimes people interfered in his affairs. He had one very great loss. But most of the time he did exactly as he pleased.

Even the strenuous trip to Missouri was pleasant. The word spread through all Kentucky that the Boones were pushing off to a new wilderness. In covered wagons, on horseback or in canoes along the streams, people went north to the Ohio River to say good-bye. Daniel, driving his cows along the bank, and Rebecca, riding in the big canoe, saw many of their old friends and met hundreds of new friends—people who had heard of Daniel Boone for years and now had a chance actually to see him!

Daniel's first big annoyance came at St. Louis. Spain then owned the great expanse of territory called Louisiana, which spread like a fan from the mouth of the Mississippi northward to the Canadian border. Spanish officials wanted people to settle in and develop this territory, and they knew that wherever Daniel Boone went, others would follow. So the Spanish governor at St. Louis organized a parade and a big reception in Daniel's honor.

Daniel did not enjoy parades and receptions in his own or anybody else's honor. He was embarrassed when people crowded around and cheered. But he suffered through the ordeal to establish good relations with the Spanish authorities.

The governor told Daniel to select about 10,000 acres for himself anywhere north of the Missouri River, and to parcel out smaller farms to each of the men who came with him. Daniel thanked the governor, and as soon as all the fancy doings were done, he pushed on into the wilds.

About sixty miles west of the confluence of the Missouri and Mississippi rivers, Daniel founded a settlement called Missouriton. There was plenty of land for everybody. Daniel and each of the men who came with him staked out a farm and built a cabin. Most of them cleared a patch of land for farming. But Daniel had no time to clear land. The hunting was too good.

At first he hunted close to the settlement. But in the fall of 1801 he went on a long hunt, taking with him a Negro boy as camp keeper. He caught only fifty beaver, probably because he spent most of his time exploring.

The next fall he and the boy went out again and ran into trouble. They had just established a comfortable camp, and Daniel had taken a few pelts, when a party of Indians charged into camp and grabbed up everything worth grabbing. They even pulled Daniel's coat off his back.

But Daniel still knew how to handle people, including Indians. He laughed at them, taunted them, and threatened them in his usual reckless, friendly manner. They decided he must have some powerful magic about him or he would be more afraid of them. They gave back most of his stuff and left him in peace.

He took about two hundred valuable beaver pelts on this hunt.

During summer seasons when he was not hunting, he acted as judge and lawmaker for the settlement. He held court under a big tree near his cabin. Here he settled land disputes and decided how wrongdoers should be punished. He knew little about law and court procedure, but he made up his laws and rules as he went along, and the people were satisfied. His law was good enough for them.

In 1803 the United States purchased the great tract of land called Louisiana, and in March of the following year, American officials took possession. Daniel's land troubles began again.

Under Spanish law a man was supposed to cultivate a part of the land he claimed. American officials said Daniel did not own any land because he had not done any cultivating. Daniel was disgusted. He wrote dignified letters to some of his influential friends in the east, asking them to take the matter up in Congress. Then he went hunting again.

During the War of 1812 a small band of Indians attacked one of the outlying cabins of the Missouriton settlement, wounding a man and three children. Daniel dressed their wounds with the skill he had acquired years before in Kentucky. A settler who watched him at this task wrote, "The old pioneer was quiet and unexcited as usual, but his lips were compressed and a fire gleamed in his eyes."

Daniel suffered the greatest loss of his life when Rebecca died in 1813. He selected a site for her grave on top of a mound overlooking the Missouri River. He felt he would soon join her there, and he always liked the top of a hill where the view was good.

About a year later he learned that the Congress of the United States had granted him a thousand acres of land in recognition of his "many eminent services" in exploring and settling the western country. At last he had a clear and undisputed title to a piece of land. He sold the land, paid his debts, and went hunting.

No one knows how far Daniel explored before and after the War of 1812. He may have gone as far as what is now Yellowstone Park. When he was eighty-two years old, he walked into Fort Osage, near where Kansas City now stands. An officer there wrote, "We have been honored by a visit from Colonel Boone, the first settler of Kentucky; he lately spent two weeks with us. . . . The colonel cannot live without being in the woods. He goes a hunting twice a year to the remotest wilderness he can reach."

Daniel wore the "dress of the roughest, poorest hunter."

During one of these hunts, a band of Osage Indians rode up to his camp and demanded that he give them his pelts. But Daniel was not in a mood to give away anything. He cocked his long rifle and aimed it at the leader of the band.

The Indians were amazed, not knowing they were dealing with the most experienced Indian fighter in the world. They had not expected trouble from an old man with long white hair. They looked at the rifle and at the old man's face and rode away.

On another of these trips, when he was far from home,

Daniel became ill. This was a new experience for him and he decided his time had come. He gave careful instructions to his boy camp keeper.

"When I die," he said, "wash me and wrap me in the cleanest blanket. Dig a hole on top of that hill and bury me there, and put poles over the grave so the wolves can't

They had not expected trouble from an old man

dig down. Then go back to the settlement and tell my kin. They'll want to dig me up and bury me beside my wife."

But a few days later Daniel felt better, got up, and picked up his rifle.

If for any reason Daniel did not feel up to a long hunt, he stayed at home and played with his grandchildren. In 1817, when he was eighty-three, he went back to Kentucky to visit old friends. Kentuckians were very proud of him by this time and held a big reception in his honor. Prominent men made speeches. But Daniel slipped away from the gathering as soon as he could.

"I dislike to be in a crowd where I have to receive so much attention," he said.

Tired of fame, he went back to Missouri to play with the children and plan another hunt.

On September 26, 1820, when he was nearly eighty-six, he died in his sleep at the home of his son Nathan and was buried beside Rebecca on the high mound.

Thus ends the story of the man Daniel Boone. He always considered himself a common man, lucky in having such a fine family but unlucky in other ways. When people honored him, he felt that they had made a mistake, because he hadn't done anything to get excited about.

He wanted a patch of land to leave to his children, so they wouldn't go hungry. He wanted a cabin where Rebecca and the children could live comfortably, and where he could stay in the summer when he was not hunting. He liked to be with people and listen to the stories they told. He could tell a few of his own.

But for himself he wanted only a couple of good rifles, a skinning knife, powder and lead and a bullet mold, and some good linen patches, and about 100,000 square miles of wild country full of bear, deer, buffalo, beaver, otter, and turkey. If Indians lived there, that was all right. He could get along with Indians.

He liked Indians unless they tried to kill his people or steal his pelts. He liked his people unless they started lawsuits over land titles.

That is the real Daniel Boone.

But the Daniel Boone of legend is a tall, lean man in a coonskin cap who discovered Kentucky and then moved west because he did not like people.

According to this legend, he was master of the wilderness and could see a sign in "a turned leaf, a blade of grass pressed down, the uneasiness of wild animals, the flight of birds."

Like most legends, this one is only partly true. Daniel was lean but not very tall. He never wore a coonskin cap. He was not the first white man to go into Kentucky, although he was the first to explore it thoroughly. He liked people. He moved west because he wanted to see the country.

It is true that he was master of the wilderness, one of the greatest scouts who ever lived. He was also master of himself. He did not display fright or anger. He never complained, but kept his troubles to himself.

But Daniel Boone will always be remembered because he has become the symbol of the pioneer, of the adventurer who must know what lies beyond the horizon. The spirit of Daniel Boone is in the boy who climbs a hill to see what is on the other side, and in the astronomer who looks through a telescope to see what is in the Milky Way.

Whenever you are tired of doing the same old thing every day—whenever you ask yourself if you have the courage to undertake some great task which you know will involve hardship and danger—then you find Daniel Boone at your elbow saying, "Come on, let's start out."

A NOTE TO *REAL* SCHOLARS

Clearing out a tangled mass of legends, modern scholars have found much authentic information about Daniel Boone, but we must still rely partly upon legends if we want to know him as a colorful human being. In a short work, intended to present Boone as a real man, a writer must use legendary material and make certain inferences which fit the known facts.

The incidents related in the first chapter are based upon the facts that the boy Daniel herded cows in the far pasture, that he made himself a throwing spear with which he hunted small game, and that Delaware Indians roamed these woods. Knowing the ways of small boys in the woods, I have told what must have happened—that Daniel crept toward a sentry crow, that he saw bear tracks, that he saw Indians. There is no historical proof that he did all of these things on one particular morning. In this chapter I have done what a dramatist or scenario writer would have to do throughout the work—invent scenes and minor incidents.

Also, elsewhere in the book, when I have put words in the mouth of Daniel Boone, I have let him speak in simple, modern, conversational style. From the few letters in Boone's own handwriting which have been preserved, we know he expressed himself simply, vigorously and bluntly, and yet his early biographers credit him with a style modeled after that of Daniel Webster. We know the substance of what Boone said on many occasions, but we do not know his exact words.

I even took the liberty of altering one generally accepted story, because it seems only partly accurate. The story is that Daniel removed the bullets from the guns of some Shawnee warriors, deliberately provoked them to fire at him, and then fooled them into thinking he caught their bullets in his shirt tail. But I'm sure that he did not even attempt to fool them in this way. The Shawnees of that time knew guns very well. A gun shooting only wadding makes a much different sound than a gun shooting a bullet, and has much less kick. As soon as the guns went off, the Shawnees knew the bullets had been removed. But the joke was still on them, because they should not have been so careless as to leave their guns unguarded.

THE AUTHOR

REAL DATES IN THE LIFE OF DANIEL BOONE

Early biographers gave many dates for Boone's birth, but according to the Boone family bible, he was born October 22, 1734, old style, which is November 2, 1734, by the modern calendar. Boone himself insisted on using the old calendar throughout his life. Dates in the following table are modern calendar dates.

1750, May 1	Boone family leave Pennsylvania home
1751 or 1752	reaches Yadkin Valley, North Carolina
1753, Dec. 29	father buys farm
1755, July 9	flees from Indians after Braddock's defeat
1756, Aug. 14	marries Rebecca Bryan
1757	son James born
1759	son Israel born
1760	daughter Susannah born
1762	daughter Jemima born
1766	daughter Lavina born
1768	daughter Rebecca born

1769	son Daniel Morgan born
1769, May 1	starts first trip to Kentucky
1769, Dec. 22	captured by Capt. Will
1770	Stuart disappears
1770, May	Squire Boone, jr., departs for the settlements leaving Daniel alone
1770	leaps into tree to escape Indians
1770, July 27	Squire returns from North Carolina
1771	Daniel and Squire go back to the Yadkin Valley
1773	son John born
1773, Sept.	Daniel starts for Kentucky with first group of settlers
1773, Oct.	son James killed by Indians
1774, May	visits James' grave
1774, summer	goes to Kentucky with Mike Stoner
1775, Mar., April	Daniel, Squire and other men go into Kentucky and establish Boonesborough
1775, May	government established for new territory of "Transylvania"
1775, June	Daniel returns to Yadkin Valley to get his family
1775, Sept.	brings family to Kentucky
1776, July	three girls captured
1777, April	Daniel wounded by Indians
1778, Feb.	captured by Blackfish
1778, Mar.	taken to Detroit, brought back to Chillicothe for adoption into tribe

1778, June	escapes, returns to Boonesborough
1778, Sept.	Blackfish lays siege
1778, autumn	Daniel goes to Yadkin Valley
1779, Oct.	Daniel, with family and others, returns and establishes Boone's Station
1780, spring	Daniel is robbed in Virginia
1780, Oct.	Daniel's brother Edward killed
1781	Daniel's son Nathan born
1781, April	British capture Daniel in Virginia
1781, Dec.	Daniel plays truant from Virginia Legislature
1782, Aug.	Battle of Blue Licks
1783 or 1784	Daniel escapes from tobacco shed
1799, Sept.	departs for Missouri
1813, Mar. 18	Rebecca dies
1820, Sept. 26	Daniel dies

INDEX

DEANE
CATE